SCEPTICISM

International Library of Philosophy and Scientific Method

A Catalogue of books already published in the
International Library of Philosophy and Scientific Method
will be found at the end of this volume.

SCEPTICISM

by

Arne Naess

NEW YORK
HUMANITIES PRESS

*First published
in the United States of America 1968
by Humanities Press Inc.
303 Park Avenue South
New York, N.Y. 10010*

© *Arne Naess 1968*

Library of Congress Catalogue Card No. 68–22775

Owing to production
delays this book was
published in 1969

Printed in Great Britain

CONTENTS

CONTENTS

CONTENTS

FOREWORD

THE present work attempts to give a concise account of sceptical philosophy in its most radical and important form. In it will be found attempts to remedy certain weaknesses in the traditional ways of describing this philosophy, and answers offered to certain arguments that have been brought against it.

I believe that there are many good reasons for investigating various forms of thinking traditionally referred to as scepticism. First, and as with many other viewpoints, the force of sceptical attitudes makes itself felt very acutely, making one at least temporarily a sceptic. Secondly, when we feel very far from scepticism it is often because we have accepted or postulated certain fundamental positions, principles, or rules, but only for the time being: from time to time these fundamentals appear arbitrary or at least less evident, obvious, or even useful, and then the attitude of sceptical 'looking around' reasserts itself. Thus, many of us are nomads in philosophy, and sceptical attitudes or doctrines are our recurring pastures.

Thirdly, sceptical philosophies, and especially Pyrrhonism as pictured by Sextus Empiricus, are mostly misunderstood and apt to be described in ways that make them appear unnecessarily crude or absurd. There is room for a more sympathetic study of the ancient texts.

The reader will find that my references to contemporary philosophers who discuss scepticism are mostly critical. This must not be taken to imply a quite general disagreement with them, let alone a negative assessment of their contributions. It is simply that discursive economy requires that I concentrate on those points on which I disagree with them, or agree only with qualifications. I should like to say here that I find many contemporary discussions admirably clear and pertinent, and perhaps especially those which I find reason to dispute on certain points.

I am grateful to the Norwegian Research Council for Science and the Humanities for a grant making it possible to carry through the historical research involved, and to Mr. Alastair Hannay for valuable assistance in revising the manuscript.

I

PYRRHO'S SCEPTICISM
ACCORDING TO
SEXTUS EMPIRICUS

I. INTRODUCTION

In this chapter I offer an account of only one special form of scepticism, the philosophical activity and view known as Pyrrhonism. Moreover, the account I give is of Pyrrhonism as represented by Sextus Empiricus. Thus, my treatment of scepticism might seem to be doubly narrow. However, there are some reasons for not attempting a more inclusive picture. One is that such presentations can already be found in textbooks on Greek philosophy and in philosophical and other reference books, and there are also a number of monographs devoted to the subject. But there is a more compelling reason too.

Apart from some very few monographs from between fifty and a hundred years ago, there are no accounts of Greek scepticism that seriously undertake the task of seeing the sceptics as they saw themselves. It is, of course, a very common experience that if one studies a philosophy closely, one becomes dissatisfied with existing accounts of it. This case, however, is a special one: the distance between what Sextus Empiricus seems to convey to his reader and the usual account we are given of what he says is altogether too great to let go unnoticed.

There is also a special reason for concentrating on Sextus's account of Pyrrhonism. As he portrays it Pyrrho's scepticism is, so far as I can judge, superior to any other variant in its consistency, its radicalness, and also in its *practical* importance for intellectually gifted persons with high ideals of sincerity and honesty. Thus Sextus's Pyrrhonism provides us with a yardstick and a fundamental framework by means of which all forms of less radical, less consistent scepticism may be measured and mapped out. I therefore invite the reader to try to understand this radical scepticism, and not be impatient with what at first sight can hardly fail to seem absurd or far-fetched.

This, then, is the motivation for our short and general account of but one of the varieties of scepticism, *Pyrrhonism as depicted by Sextus Empiricus.*

The sources, as with all philosophical classics, lend themselves to different interpretations, and I do not wish to try to convince the reader that my own interpretation is the only one that can be constructed on an historical basis. But I think that many will agree that the interpretation I give presents the sceptic (here in the sense of the Pyrrhonist as pictured by Sextus) as less inconsistent or preposterous in his claims than he is made to appear in some of the most widely read accounts.

2. SHORT ACCOUNT OF SEXTUS'S PYRRHONISM

Much learned historical work has been undertaken to find out which sceptics taught what. I shall try neither to add to nor subtract from the conclusions of historians of philosophy on this point. The decisive thing to note is that the only extant work by a Greek sceptic is that of Sextus Empiricus. The study of Greek scepticism must therefore in the main be a study of his texts.

There are, it is true, reasons to suspect that Sextus is not altogether accurate in what he says about other sceptics, that Pyrrho in particular might not have approved of all of Sextus's references to him. But I shall not be concerned with this question; instead I shall try to give a summary account of Pyrrhonism as depicted by Sextus in his work *Outlines of Pyrrhonism.* What marginal notes and exclamations Pyrrho himself would have put into a copy of Sextus's *Outlines* is an intriguing topic for speculation. The account I shall give is something that can be assessed and tested by studying the actual texts by Sextus. In what follows, 'Pyrrhonism' and 'scepticism' will be used as shorthand for 'Pyrrhonism as pictured by Sextus'.

But first, in order to clear up some ambiguities, a few remarks on the use of the term 'scepticism'. The term is used in many ways, which can be distinguished by separating four dimensions of variation:

1. *Comprehensiveness.* 'Scepticism' is often used as short for 're-ligious scepticism', for 'ethical scepticism', or for some other non-total field of human concern. The most comprehensive kind of

philosophical scepticism covers all fields of articulated cognition or discursive thinking. Pyrrhonism belongs to that kind.

2. *Intensity.* If a philosopher thinks we are able at least sometimes to distinguish the more probable from the less, but not the true from the probable, or the false from the improbable, he is often called 'sceptical'. But those philosophers are also sometimes said to be sceptics who suggest that the more probable can never be distinguished from the less. The difference may be said to be one of intensity.

3. *Self-reference.* If a thinker states that nothing can be known, the question arises whether he thinks he can know that he cannot know anything. If he answers Yes, his statement of his doctrine does not refer to a class containing that same statement as a member. If he answers No, we may say the statement is intended to include itself in its reference. Sometimes the former position is called 'Academic' or 'Dogmatic' and distinguished from the latter. This is the terminology I shall adopt. (It may of course be disputed whether this third dimension, of self-reference, is independent of the first and second. It is in any case convenient to treat the question of self-reference as a unique one.)

4. *Articulateness.* As a professional philosopher the sceptic must articulate his scepticism, preferably in words. The great sceptics of the classical Greek tradition, which lasted about five and a half centuries, were not only masters of sceptical verbal articulation but also sceptical in their non-verbal attitudes. In the history of ideas and in general cultural history, non-verbal attitudes also count. A person may be termed a sceptic even if he does not express his bent of mind verbally.

For our own purposes the best way of identifying scepticism is to follow Sextus in his narrative of how (certain) gifted persons develop by stages into mature sceptics. Seven points characterize the development:

1. Faced with 'contradictions' in things and with philosophers who contradict one another, gifted people become frustrated and undecided, and set out to discover for themselves what is true and what is false. They are led to consider all kinds of doctrines and arguments in the hope of restoring their peace of mind.[1]

---

[1] See Sextus Empiricus, *Outlines of Pyrrhonism*, Bk. I, Sects. 12 and 26. (In all references to this work Arabic figures refer to sections unless explicitly to chapters.) The German translation by Eugen Pappenheim of Bk. I, 12, is very good at this

2. Those of them who investigate matters systematically eventually become philosophers. As such they fall into one of the following three main classes: those who claim that they have found at least one truth, those who claim that truth *cannot* be found in any matter, and those who neither claim that they have found at least one truth nor claim to *know* that truth cannot be found, but persist in their seeking.[1]

These three groups are respectively called the Dogmatists, the Academicians and the Sceptics. (The first two are also called dogmatic in a wider sense.) It is important to note here that in contemporary Anglo-American professional philosophy the sceptic is identified with the person who positively denies that one may know anything for certain. That is, the sceptic is identified with what Sextus calls the Academician. The Academician takes active part in philosophical discussion, maintaining a definite position, a standpoint; the sceptic in the sense of Sextus has no position, as we shall see. Although he throws arguments into the discussion, he takes no part in it. Although he confronts the dogmatist with counterarguments, he does so without accepting any of them as true or valid.

3. The personal development of the sceptic is of a peculiar kind: he finds that to any *pro*-argument for a doctrine or proposition there can be found an at least equally strong *contra*-argument, or that, summing up pro's and con's, the arguments balance one another. Or, to be more accurate, he finds no better grounds for accepting the arguments in favour of the doctrine than for accepting those against it.[2] These statements require careful interpretation.

It would be a misunderstanding with grave consequences, for example, to attribute to the Pyrrhonist a *principle* in the sense of a general rule, of opposing all arguments with equally strong arguments. Such a principle can only be conceived to hold good in general if one is sure, or can take it for granted, that there are always such arguments to be found. But, as will become clearer

[1] Bk. I, 1–3.
[2] See Bk. I, 8, 10, 12, 26.

point: 'Hochbegabte Menschen nämlich kamen, beirrt durch die Ungleichmässigkeit in den Dingen und unentschieden, welchen von ihnen sie sich mehr fügen sollten, dahin, zu suchen, was wahr sei bei den Dingen und was falsch, um in Folge der Entscheidung hierüber unbeirrt zu sein.' *Sextus Empiricus, Pyrrhoneïsche Grundzüge* (Erich Koschny, Leipzig, 1877), p. 26.

later, whether this is the case is a question the Pyrrhonist leaves open. Otherwise he would side with the Academicians.[1]

Thus, the developing sceptic (or: the sceptic *in statu nascendi*) has no prejudice in favour of counterarguments. He does not look more intently for *contra*- than for *pro*-arguments. It just so happens that he finds that arguments balance one another. Or, to be more exact, it so happens that he does not find a sufficient weight either *pro* or *contra* to justify a decision about what is true, or even about what is more probable. In order to stress his lack of conclusions, he prudently uses the past tense: he has not, up to now, found anything that decisively disturbs the balance between *pro* and *contra*, that disturbs his general *isosthenia* or state of mental suspense.[2]

4. The corresponding psychological phase in the making of a mature sceptic is the gradual development of a deeply entrenched bent of mind, a state of suspension of judgment, or *epoché*. The mature sceptic decides neither for the positive nor for the negative in relation to any doctrine, but allows both possibilities to stand open. The suspension is a form of mental rest (quietude, repose, immobility, stability [*stasis dianoias*]). The suspension slowly develops into a firmly based bent of mind.[3]

5. To his surprise he eventually finds that *epoché* leads to, or is accompanied by, just that peace of mind (*ataraxia*) which he set out to achieve by finding truth.[4]

The mature sceptic will not, of course, claim that there is a necessary connection between *epoché* and *ataraxia*.

6. The mature sceptic obeys or follows the ordinary or normal rules of his community. He is guided, but not determined, by nature, traditions, laws, and customs. He may instruct himself in some skill or other and adopt one, perhaps medicine, professionally.[5]

7. The mature sceptic is still a seeker. He does not claim to

---

[1] In this connection the second last sentence of Bk. I, 12, is important. R. G. Bury (*Outlines of Pyrrhonism* [Loeb Classical Library, W. Heinemann, London, 1933]) translates: 'The main basic principle of the Sceptic system is that of opposing to every proposition an equal proposition . . .' (p. 9). But here we should first of all reject the term 'system'. Secondly, the term 'basic principle' somewhat unhappily suggests a rule or proposition claimed to be valid. Thirdly, an impression of deliberate policy is conveyed by talking of a principle of doing so-and-so. Pappenheim has avoided most of these unsceptical suggestions, translating *systaseos arché* as *des Verharrens Anfang*: 'Des skeptischen Verharrens Anfang (Grundprincip) aber ist hauptsächlich, dass jeder Rede eine gleiche Rede gegenübersteht.' p. 26.

[2] Bk. I, 190, 200.   [3] Bk. I, 8, 10, 196, 205.
[4] Bk. I, 8, 10, 12, 17, 28–30.   [5] Bk. I, 17, 22–30, 226–7, 230–1, 237–8.

know that truth cannot be found in any matter. So, he is prepared to investigate and evaluate any new argument in relation to any conclusion. He leaves all questions open, but without leaving the question. He has, however, given up his original, ultimate aim of gaining peace of mind by finding truth, because it so happened that he came by peace of mind in another way.

To sum up, then, scepticism is neither a doctrine nor a system of rules of life positively claimed to bring peace of mind. The mature sceptic is a philosopher who, like the early Socrates and like many influential philosophers of our own time, makes no philosophical assertions. The most adequate exposition of the philosophy of the mature sceptic is to give an account or narrative of his life in the way Sextus does. However, since Sextus the metasceptic is the same person as Sextus the sceptic, he explicitly denies that he claims the (objective) truth of any of the statements of the narrative. Not that the sceptic cannot allow himself to *say* anything, and must inhibit any tendency to do so. If he feels like it he may express what is in his mind, and sometimes this will result in long narratives. His ways of verbal announcement are many, but they do not include assertion of truth.

Having attained peace of mind (*ataraxia*) by suspending judgment (*epoché*) and having reached general suspension of judgment by *isosthenia*, the sceptic is inclined to try to preserve *isosthenia*, that is, to look for counterarguments and countercounterarguments. A natural expectation will be built up that he will in this way retain his general suspension of mind. And he will be inclined to try to help others who are not yet, but seem to be on the way to becoming, mature sceptics.

In certain kinds of situations those following the sceptical way make use of *a set of maxims*, or sayings, often called sceptical, such as 'Arguments and counterarguments balance each other'. But here the claim ordinarily intended when asserting something is not made; rather, such maxims are to be taken as symptomatic of the state of the sceptical mind. Thus the maxim 'No statement is true' is, according to Sextus, self-defeating as an *assertion*: if it is true, then it is false. He therefore does not feel inclined to *assert* that knowledge cannot be reached, or to venture any of the other sayings frequently taken to be expressions of a *doctrine* of scepticism.

In short, although the sceptical philosophy is verbally articulated in a most careful way, among the many ways of using language there is one that the sceptic studiously avoids: the assertive.

In what follows we shall adopt the above seven-point definition of scepticism. Thus it will be a matter of definition that the mature sceptic has peace of mind. Indeed, all traits mentioned in the seven points will belong to the sceptic by definition. What can fruitfully be discussed, therefore, is, among other things, the conditions and likelihood of the seven-point development, the stability of scepticism as a bent of mind and way of life. This, as we shall see later, is the same as to discuss the possibility of a radical scepticism.

3. THE SCEPTICAL WAYS OF ANNOUNCEMENT

Sextus, then, is not a philosopher with doctrines. He will not admit to having any definite opinion as to the truth or falsity of any proposition. But in that case how are his own utterances (*fonai*) to be interpreted? What uses of language are they? And what ways has he of *announcing*, this being the function Sextus attributes to those of his utterances which the uninstructed reader would take to assert truth, to express propositions?

Sextus makes use of a great variety of terms in contrasting his own ways of announcing with those of the dogmatists.

I shall first mention some of those used in the opening chapters of *Outlines of Pyrrhonism*.

1. *To report as a chronicler.* At the end of the first chapter he says that in what follows he does not affirm the truth of what he says, but only *reports as a chronicler* how things appear to him at the moment of writing.

The crucial expression here is '*historikós apangellomen*'.[1]

Even someone who is, in the usual sense of the word, merely a reporter of what appears to him at the moment to be the case would claim truth for his account of the *appearances*. He would affirm that this and not something else is how it *really* 'strikes him' at the moment. Later we shall see how Sextus meets this complication. In fact he virtually retracts the view that the sceptic uses language in the same ways as a chronicler or reporter. In other words, the first special characterization of the sceptical way of announcement is not a very happy one.

[1] For study of the use of *apangello* and related words see especially Chaps, 23, 25, and 27 of Bk. I.

2. *To utter.* In Chapter II Sextus declares that later on in the book he will give an account of how or in what sense the sceptic adopts what he, the sceptic, 'shows forth' or 'displays in words'. These somewhat peculiar expressions I use only provisionally. In fact the term Sextus adopts is one that he often uses in connection with statements of doctrine—*apofasis.* One important complex expression is *skeptikai apofaseis.* Bury translates this 'sceptic formulae', Pappenheim 'skeptische Aussagen'. However, when Sextus comes to the passages in question, he does not use the dangerous word *apofasis;* instead he consistently uses *foné,* 'utterance'. This term appears in Stoic and other logical texts as in contradistinction to *lekton* (that which is [or might be] signified by the utterance);[1] its most elementary meaning is 'sound', and by using this term, Sextus avoids contamination with doctrinal ways of announcement. He leaves it open as to what use of language is realized: *foné* is a highly non-committal word.

3. *To acquiesce in and accept (in words) what appears.* The sceptic does not oppose what appears to him, but acquiesces (*eudokeo*) in it. The term *eu-dokeo* contains *dokeo* ('I opine', etc.), but apart from meaning '*think* well of', it can also mean 'accept', 'say yes to', in a non-cognitive way. He accepts (*synkatatithémi,* assent to) what, involuntarily or by necessity, appears to him (Bk. I, 13). Thus, when feeling hot or cold, he will not say that it does *not* seem hot or cold to him.

From these formulations one can gather that Sextus looks upon some or all of the sceptic's utterances as more or less *caused* by states of perception[2] which are forced upon him. When saying 'I feel cold', the sceptic does not make an assertion *about* something, he assents *to* something. Although what he says *can* be construed as an assertion, it is not in the sense in which to assert something is to positively take a stand for rather than against; he is not asserting *rather than* denying; he does not *oppose* an impulse towards not saying it. He will neither affirm nor deny 'It now seems hot (cold) to me' as a proposition.

4. *The sceptical formulae or phrases.* Sextus divides what the sceptic talks about into two classes, the evident (*délon*) and the non-evident (*adélon*). The 'immediate' and the 'mediate' may be better translations. What is said under 3 above (*Outlines,* Bk. I,

---

[1] Ten occurrences of *foné* are found in four important chapters (7, 8, 19, 28) of the *Outlines,* Bk. I, 14, 15, 187, 188, 191, 207.

[2] If 'all utterances', then 'perception' must be taken in a rather wide sense.

13) holds for the evident ('I feel cold', etc.). But the sceptic also utters his famous 'sceptical phrases'. These make up either a subclass or a total class of his own sayings about non-evident things, such as arguments.

That the sceptic does not intend to assert something, to state that something is the case, when uttering his sceptical phrases, is clearly, explicitly, and repeatedly stated by Sextus himself. It would be of no avail to assert them, says Sextus, because each one 'cancels itself', 'strikes itself out' (*perigrafo*). Thus even 'Not more this than that', which is said when comparing the force of argument with that of counterargument, is meant to apply universally; it too cancels itself out, just like the (non-sceptical) phrase 'Nothing is true'. The same applies to 'I do not decide (determine the truth value of) anything', because according to it, I do not even decide that I decide nothing.

Incidentally, neither 'Nothing is true' nor 'All is false', mentioned here (*Outlines*, Bk. I, 14), is included among the sceptical phrases.

5. *To put forward.* Of the sceptical formulae, Sextus says that they are *put* (set) *forward* (*profero*).[1] They are put before the dogmatist and used for didactic purposes among sceptics during their training, not to teach sceptical theorems (they do not exist) but to suggest the state of mind of the sceptic when approached by dogmatists. Their function would resemble that of certain standard exclamations like 'Well, I never!', 'Take your time!', 'Be careful!', etc.

6. Sextus uses such words as '*perhaps*', '*presumably*', '*it seems*' out of standard context. That is, where he puts them they would be badly placed if it were not that they were to remind the reader that 'this is not to be taken as an assertion'. The book's very opening sentence has an unnatural 'it seems': 'Those who seek, it seems, either find what they are looking for, or reject the (possibility of) finding it, and deny that it can be grasped, or go on searching.' Most likely this is meant to be an exhaustive classification: at least Sextus suggests nothing that could be argued against it. The 'it seems' serves to indicate that the main sentence is intended to function not as an assertion of a true proposition but as an utterance of some other kind. On the other hand, Sextus intends that the dogmatist should be able to evaluate the proposition that the sentence *can* be intended to express, even though it did not happen to be thus intended by the sceptic.

---

[1] The dogmatist also 'puts forward' but 'with affirmation' (Bk. I, 197).

7. *To say something indicative of our state of mind* (how we feel about things) (Bk. I, 197). Sextus says about one of the sceptical phrases, namely 'I determine nothing', that it is not meant as an affirmation; rather it is a sound (*foné*, utterance) indicative of the sceptic's state (of mind).[1] There are two interpretations of 'indicative' that can be applied in this context: 'deliberately intended to be indicative' and 'indicative as a matter of fact.' The latter fits in best with the general attitude of the sceptic.

8. *Talking loosely.* One may talk without presupposing any definite conceptual frame of reference, taking 'conceptual' here in a rather narrow sense, not in the broad way in which children conceptualize as soon as they learn to use everyday abstract terms. As examples of conceptualization, Sextus mostly refers to explicit definitions or closed systems of propositions. We may think of a conceptual framework or frame of reference, therefore, as a system of definitions providing clear-cut rules of interpretation, at least for certain basic terms. Obvious examples of such terms nowadays would be 'true', 'truth', 'fact', and 'proposition'. Philosophers who define these terms become involved in the choice or development of complicated conceptual structures, just as do biologists in defining 'life', and anthropologists in defining 'man'. Where, as in most cases, the terms in these structures are taken from everyday language, they are given clearly delimited meanings which contrast with their more loose employment in ordinary contexts. In their explicitly delimited use terms are applied, and propositions expressed by means of them accepted or rejected, according to the explicit commitments of the system. In their 'ordinary' use no such commitments are intended, no choice among the alternative structures is made. Thus if I say 'I see a man coming', I may do so without having any definition of man (for example, Plato's) in mind; in speaking loosely, no such definition need be presupposed. Consequently if I am asked to state exactly what my proposition is, I may answer, 'Honestly, as far as I can judge, I did not have anything definite in mind. As regards "man", I never saw a definition I felt was a good one; on the other hand, I never really felt the need of a definition'.

The 'loose talk' Sextus engages in is in this way philosophically uncommitted talk, talk with rather little definiteness of intention

---

[1] Pappenheim translates very well: 'eine Redensart, welche unseren Zustand kundthut' (p. 71).

relative to questions which are not of an everyday nature, or which presuppose explicit conceptual frameworks. Its low degree of definiteness in fact renders it *incapable of location* with respect to a conceptual system or frame which presupposes higher definiteness, and an utterance such as 'I see a man coming' may be perfectly appropriate even if it lacks a definiteness of intention such as would render it classifiable in relation to theological, existential, biological, or anthropological definitions of man. The notion of the degree of a term's definiteness of intention will be elaborated later (see Chap. 4, Sect. 9). But provisionally we can identify what is meant by noting that in talking about something not only do we use words that are inherently indeterminate or ambiguous, in that they can be used on different occasions to say different things, but also on any particular occasion we may mean neither one nor another of a number of non-synonymous interpretations of the words we use. Roughly, one utterance has less definiteness of intention than another if among a set of possible, non-synonymous interpretations common to both utterances, it makes fewer discriminations than the other utterance. A 'loose' expression is one that makes no discriminations in terms of explicit conceptual frameworks.

The Greek adverbs *adiaforos* and *adoxastos* are the main terms used by Sextus to suggest the peculiar looseness with which the sceptic puts forth the sentences by means of which he expresses his mind.[1]

Some of the apparently most absurd utterances thrown into dogmatic debate by sceptics acquire sense if interpreted in relation to definite conceptual frameworks. Consider, for instance, phrases relating to non-existence, such as 'Man does not exist', 'There is no such thing as position in space', 'No teacher exists', and the like. We may assume the sceptic to intend expressions like these in relation to particular frameworks (those of the discussions he is witness to).

9. *Giving a message.* There are other forms of giving a message than plain reporting 'as a chronicler'. Sextus uses a word (*apangellomai*) that leaves the question of technique of mediation open. The word may even cover utterances that the sceptic makes involuntarily—when he 'accepts' the appearances.

10. *Saying things.* Sextus lets the sceptic 'say' (*fémi*) this or that

[1] For some important occurrences of *adoxastos* see Bk. I, 15, 23, 24; Bk. II, 13. And of *adiaforos*, Bk. I, 195, 207.

in contexts where dogmatists would usually 'state' or 'assert' (using *lego*, etc.).

11. *Inclination to believe.* Sextus rejects probabilism, but sometimes uses terms to designate the inclination to believe one proposition rather than another (*pithanos* and *peitho*; see, e.g., *Against the Logicians*, Bk. II, 473, 475). These 'natural' inclinations he takes to be, in mature sceptics, states of mind of a transitory kind.

4. THE DOGMATIC WAYS OF ANNOUNCEMENT

1. *To opine.* Academic philosophers, says Sextus, in the opening section of the *Outlines*, have the opinion (opine, *dokeo*) that truth *cannot* be grasped, that it is inapprehensible (*akataléptos*).

In general, to put forth as an opinion, 'to opine', is treated by Sextus as a non-sceptical way of announcement. It suggests that what one says is at least nearer the truth than the negation of what one says.[1]

2. *To grasp (as true).* To say 'I found that *p*', 'I grasped that *p*', 'I discovered that *p*', and the like is, even more than 'I opine that *p*', to use a dogmatic way of announcement (*Outlines*, Chap. 1).

Sextus says that the Academician holds the opinion that he has *grasped* at least one truth, one true proposition, namely that there is not a single proposition (except this) the truth of which can be grasped.

As to this grasping, the basic metaphor seems to be that of getting a firm hold of something and keeping it securely in one's grasp.

3. *To affirm the certainty of what one says* (e.g. Bk. I, 4). The Greek term here, *diabebaioumai*, is frequently used by Sextus (on behalf of the dogmatists). In denying that what it expresses has ever found a place in his own life, he may be said to be rejecting all claims of certainty, all guaranteeing (that it is so), giving assurance, or vouching, at least as far as *he* is concerned, relative to the truth of propositions. He does not predict that it will always be so, or that it must be so (as does the Academician). Even less does he claim that one can never, or should never, be certain, feel certain, have confidence.

If one says explicitly 'It is certain that *p*', the prefix indicates

---

[1] Nevertheless, Sextus sometimes uses the term 'to opine' when referring to his own (or to sceptical) utterances (see Bk. I, 4, 17). In Bk. I, 19, the reflexive 'they seem to me' is used.

the kind of claim made about '*p*': it is one that includes the truth claim. Sextus means his comments to cover also cases in which the speaker manages to convey by other means that he holds *p* to be certain. Indeed, this applies to all the instances mentioned here: they cover not only the uses of *certain phrases* to express certain claims but also the claims themselves, however expressed.

4. *To posit as true, real or really existent.* In opposing dogmatic opinions to one another, and saying that none is more credible than any other, Sextus says that the sceptic takes nothing for granted as true or real. The expression he uses here (*tithémi hós hyparchon*) probably implies truth or at least probability, whereas to pose or posit (*tithémi*) does not.

5. *To affirm one's conviction that what one says is true* (e.g. Bk. I, 18). Sextus explains that the sceptic deals with questions concerning nature and essence in order to oppose (fight) dogmatic positions, not in order to say things with firm (certain) belief (*meta bebaiou peismatos*).

6. To say *what a thing is by nature, in itself* or *in its essence* (Bk. I, 20). Honey, says Sextus, seems sweet to us; we grant this, but whether honey *is* sweet, that is sweet by nature, in its essence, is a subject for investigation. The honey's sweetness is not appearance but something postulated on the basis of appearance.

7. *To settle* (Bk. I, 197). Sextus defines 'to settle' (*horizo*) in the relevant contexts not simply as to say something but to put forward something non-evident with affirmation (*synkatathésis*).

Bury translates the Greek word by 'to determine'. In Latin translations we usually find 'determinare'. *To settle* is a common meaning of 'horizo' however, and it suits the text, which 'determine' does not, either in the sense of 'causally determine' or that of 'define'.

8. *More worthy of belief.* Among conflicting judgments no one is more worthy of belief (*pistoteros*) than any other. Although, as we have noted, Sextus does not adhere to any probabilism, some of the terms he uses may be translated by 'probable', but it is better to refer generally to inclination towards belief.

In conclusion, then, one may say that some phrases are taken to be exclusively sceptical, others to be exclusively dogmatic, and a third group comprises phrases belonging to both groups, but with different shades of meaning. But it is important to point out that the mere isolated use of a phrase with either sceptical or dogmatic intent does not in itself mean that the user is a sceptic or a dogmatist. There is also a time factor to take into account. Psychologically, scepticism must be considered a stable disposition, even if a momentary state of mind may hide it and even be inconsistent with it. Thus, a phlegmatic man may become momentarily agitated, a mild man succumb to anger. Dispositions, however strong, are in this respect different from certain other states: the mentally blind, for example, may, under special circumstances, come to 'see the light' in a way which has no parallel with the physically blind. Similarly, the sceptic may, under special circumstances, find something to be undeniably true, indubitable, absolutely certain. He does not then *suddenly* cease to be a mature, consistent sceptic. Only if the convictions persist does he leave the brotherhood of sceptics.

These reflections call to mind a passage in Hume's *Treatise* in which the author apologizes for his very frequent lapses into a highly dogmatic style:

'It is easier to forbear all examination and inquiry, than to check ourselves in so natural a propensity, and guard against that assurance, which always arises from an exact and full survey of an object. On such an occasion we are apt not only to forget our scepticism, but even our modesty too; and make use of such terms as these, *it is evident, it is certain, it is undeniable*; which a due deference to the public ought, perhaps, to prevent. I may have fallen into this fault after the example of others; but I here enter a *caveat* against any objections, which may be offered on that head; and declare that such expressions were extorted from me by the present view of the object, and imply no dogmatical spirit, nor conceited idea of my own judgment, which are sentiments that I am sensible can become nobody, and a sceptic still less than any other.'[1]

In assessing the extent of Hume's scepticism we should perhaps keep his *caveat* in mind, though one does so with certain reservations after reading Sextus Empiricus, who himself very rarely succumbs to dogmatic expressions. Certainly the style of 'the greatest sceptic of modern time' is highly dogmatic in its use of extreme terms and its tendency to bring readers precipitately to far-reaching conclusions. One might have expected a publishing sceptic to tone down his antisceptical expressions, when revising his manuscripts or during proof-reading, but Hume gives little evidence of that. How, for example, could a sceptic conclude his

[1] *A Treatise of Human Nature*, Bk. I, Pt. 4 (Everyman's Library Edition [J. M. Dent & Sons, London, 1911]), Vol. I, p. 258.

ethical speculations with the sentence, 'Thus, upon the whole, I am hopeful that nothing is wanting to an accurate proof of this system of ethics'?[1]

There is, of course, nothing inconsistent in entertaining or expressing such a hope, but at the same time it is a hope to be rid of scepticism. Indeed, even the hope that one's system is more probable than just one other system envisages an end to one's Pyrrhonian or, for that matter, one's Academic scepticism. In order to understand the dogmatic style it is perhaps important to stress the least radical versions of the dogmatist's epistemological 'scepticism', his probabilism, which permits very high, objective probabilities to be reached.

5. NEUTRALITY TOWARDS SUBJECTIVIST PHENOMENALISM

From a close inspection of the way of the sceptic, it is clear that he tends to avoid commitment to conceptualizations or conceptual frameworks; he will therefore tend to avoid any intellectualization of trust, confidence, and belief *in terms of the truth of propositions* within such frameworks.

Pyrrho's philosophy might therefore be called 'anticonceptual', because his doubt concerning intellectual abstractions is so profound that he ends up without an explicit conceptual framework of his own. Pyrrho limits himself to undermining the conceptual frameworks of the dogmatists, without erecting any new one.

Many of the sentences and phrases used by Sextus, however, suggest adherence to a kind of phenomenalist and subjectivist position that we associate with the name of Descartes. If this were so, scepticism would be a kind of doctrinal philosophy; it would contain as an integral part a specific ontology, and it would adhere to a conceptual framework which allowed it to provide answers

---

[1] *Ibid.*, Bk. III, Pt. 3, (Everyman ed. Vol. II, p. 310). Whereas considerations of style may have perverted Hume's argumentation in a dogmatic direction (or did he perhaps wish to convert the reader to a system?), the dictates of intellectual sincerity can sometimes pervert the style of the sceptic. In the writings of Ingemund Gullvåg, a contemporary sceptic, repeated expressions of uncertainty and perplexity leave the reader wandering in a structureless plain of if's, presumably's, and perhaps's (cf. his 'Scepticism and Absurdity', *Inquiry*, Vol. 7 [1964], No. 2). One wonders how many important manuscripts by sceptics have remained unpublished because they ultimately led nowhere. Hume's writings are eminently readable in part because of the provoking dogmatism of their style and the highly interesting general conclusions that crop up in every chapter.

to questions with a high degree of definiteness of intention. It must therefore be an important part of the exegesis of our texts to see whether such a classification can be avoided without strain.

Occurrences of *fainomai* in forms other than the famous participle *fainomenon*, are plentiful. In most cases they have a rather general meaning, for example, 'it seems', 'it seems to me', 'so it appears', 'apparently', and 'so it appears to us'. What it is that appears, or seems, may be of very different kinds. At its very first occurrence, that which is said 'to appear to us' is *that Pyrrho applied himself to scepticism more thoroughly and conspicuously than his predecessors.*[1] At another place Sextus says that the sceptic uses the phrase 'I suspend judgment' to indicate that things *appear* equal as regards credibility and incredibility. In other connections these 'things' are defined as arguments; thus certain properties of arguments or of attitudes towards arguments are said to appear in certain ways. Quite often *fainetai* occurs where one would normally expect *esti* (etc.), that is, instead of 'is'. Something is said to appear, or appear so-and-so, in contrast to saying that it *is* so-and-so.

Used in this way, it is clear that, conceptually, *fainetai* ('it seems') does not imply that what seems must be sense-data, sense-impressions, subjective states, or the like. There are no definite limits to what can be said to appear and to appear so-and-so.

Subjectivity enters only in the sense that the sceptic does not claim truth, certainty, objective validity, or existence, but stresses that what he says is what *he* says and that it bears witness to *his* state of mind *at that moment*. That is, he might say something different later or may have said something different in the past. It is what *appears* to him that guides him in his daily life, not hypotheses or convictions about what is true.

Accordingly, when the sceptic says 'sweet', 'this is sweet', or 'honey, sweet', and so on, just as he does not intend to assert that honey as such, as the object perceived by him and others, *is* sweet, in the sense of having that property by nature, so neither does he intend to stress that what he speaks about is a sense-impression of sweetness, as opposed to an object causing or conditioning the sense-impression.

The best interpretation seems to me to represent the sceptic as having a definiteness of intention no greater than that which we

[1] *Outlines*, Bk. I, 7, *Fainesthai hēmin.*

have in daily life when saying, for example, 'honey, mm, yes, sweet', that is, a definiteness not great enough to say that we intend to talk about a subjective impression rather than about an intersubjective object, or vice versa. Confronted, therefore, with the philosopher's question Is the sweetness in you or in the honey?, the sceptic can already apply his suspension of judgment. He does *not* side with the phenomenalist or subjectivist who answers that sweetness is in the mind or consciousness, or is only a phenomenon without its counterpart in the object, and so forth.

There are, admittedly, certain terms used by Sextus that are often translated in such a way that the charge of phenomenalism and subjectivism seems to stick.[1] But if one takes these terms one by one it is plain, I think, that no such translations are strictly needed, and that even if certain terms are used which in *philosophy* generally express subjectivism, they need not do so in an everyday vocabulary. Thus, 'feel', in 'This is how I feel about it' need be no more subjectivist than 'So it seems to me'.

A further complication arises, however, from the use of expressions which do seem to suggest that the sceptic accepts the philosophical dualism between an external world or reality and internal states of consciousness, and consciously limits himself to introspection. But the term translated by 'external' (*exóthen*, Bk. I, 15) occurs in a context which does not imply that philosophical distinction. Two things are contrasted: giving a message concerning one's state of mind (*sein eigener Zustand* [Pappenheim]) and affirming with certainty something about its grounds, i.e. something outside the state of mind and therefore not identical with it.

In this terminology anything beyond a present state of mind would count as 'external' to this state, even if it was another state of mind, for instance, a belief one had as a child. There is no implication of externality in the sense of an external versus an introspected world.

As regards 'state of mind', the everyday use of this expression does not imply any philosophical concept of states of consciousness. Sextus uses the term (*pathos*) for all that seems, including how one feels about certain arguments.

How the ideals of historians of philosophy change! To R. D. Hicks, writing in 1910, the existence of a real world behind consciousness seemed to be a fundamental problem and neglect of it a tremendous handicap.

[1] E.g. *Ta aisthéta* (Bk. I, 9), *fantasia* (Bk. I, 13), and *pathos* (Bk. I, 13).

'The scepticism of antiquity busied itself with the problem of knowledge. But when compared with cognate inquiries in modern philosophy, it appears in its scope and range almost ludicrously tentative, jejune, and superficial. That the object of cognition was external reality, nay more, that it was material reality, was not in that age seriously questioned. No one ever challenged the existence of a real world of things lying behind the phenomena of which we are conscious.'[1]

The implied criticism is that although Berkeleyan idealism (as traditionally conceived) had not yet been developed, a contemporary of Sextus should none the less have taken account of it. But there is no reason why sceptics should proffer arguments against distinctions and positions not yet developed by any dogmatists. And in any case, in suspending judgment about propositions concerning things (e.g. honey) which are said to have certain qualities (e.g. colours, tastes), the Pyrrhonist has made it sufficiently clear just how he would react both to an assertion and to a denial of an external world.[2]

The scope of Karl Jaspers's penetrating *Psychologie der Weltanschauungen* leads one to expect a broad treatment of a variety of sceptical attitudes. But although there is some variety, it is unfortunately all mixed up with kinds of nihilism. Nietzsche and reactions to Nietzsche dominate Jaspers's approach. Pyrrho's answer to the question 'How is the world?', his world view (*Weltbild*), is itemized in seven dogmatic and sweeping statements.[3] One of these is that we do not know and cannot know how the world is. Others represent Pyrrho as a phenomenalist and subjectivist in the modern philosophical sense. All in all, the sceptic according to Jaspers is a rather pitiable creature to be characterized mainly by what he lacks.

In the first book of *Against the Logicians*, Sections 190–9, Sextus gives a detailed and very clear account of the Cyrenaic position. It is a marked subjectivism, according to which one may

[1] *Stoic and Epicurean* (Longmans, London, 1910), pp. 312–13.

[2] Hicks wrote in 1910, but as recently as 1964 there have been writers who think that scepticism essentially concerns itself with the belief in an external or material world. The *Dictionnaire de la philosophie*, Libraire Larousse, says some quite astonishing things: 'Hegel a distingué, d'une manière très lumineuse: 1° le *scepticisme antique* (Pyrrhon, Aenésidème), qui consiste à douter de la réalité du monde extérieur et à croire néanmoins en la réalité d'un monde spirituel, et l'existence de Dieu; 2°, le *scepticisme moderne* (positivisme, scientisme), qui consiste à ne croire que ses sens, à affirmer la seule réalité du monde matériel et à douter de Dieu. Le Philosophe Berkeley rentrerait dans la première catégorie, Auguste Comte dans la seconde.'

[3] *Psychologie der Weltanschauungen* (4th edn., Springer Verlag, Berlin, 1954), p. 297.

infallibly make judgments about feelings (in the old sense of affective states). We can state with infallible certainty that we sense whiteness or sweetness, but we cannot grasp the objects producing these feelings or tell whether they are white or sweet. Feeling is the criterion: truths can be grasped, but only in so far as they describe feelings. Significantly, however, Sextus takes this doctrine to be an example of a dogmatic solution to the problem of a criterion of knowledge. That is, Sextus himself does not adhere to any of these solutions; he uses them as counterarguments. And he also brings arguments against the position that there can be a criterion.

It is therefore safe to conclude that scepticism according to Sextus does not embrace the subjectivism of the Cyrenaics or any other sect. Feelings, appearances, sensations are not capable of furnishing a criterion of truth and validity, not even for a proposition which itself only describes an affection, appearance, or sensation.

So much is clear from the lengthy discussion by Sextus of criteria of truth and validity. Nevertheless there are passages in the *Outlines* which are liable to be misunderstood. Thus, in one place Sextus seems to confirm that only one's own states of mind can be 'grasped'.[1] What one should do in such cases, however, is to give the passage an interpretation consistent with the rejection of any criterion, not to take it as proof of his belief in introspective certainty and knowledge.

Our conclusion, then, is this:

Scepticism, if defined by the seven-point account of its genesis, far from implying modern philosophical subjectivism, introspectivism, or phenomenalism, is at once more general, formal, and dialectical. In fact, the sceptic preserves his neutrality by not transcending certain everyday distinctions which may, but need not, lead to just such systems if worked out in relation to precise conceptual frameworks.

Indeed, it might be said that Sextus Empiricus's great contribution to thought was his indication of scepticism as a way of life, a way in which the embrace of doctrine is systematically avoided. If it is easy, as it has been customary, to praise him simply as an early expounder of more recent doctrines, or to see him simply as a useful source of philosophical theories, it is because one forgets or fails to see that these views were simply meant to be thrown in

[1] *Outlines*, Bk. I, 215.

to counter doctrines likely to be held by his contemporaries. Consider, for example, R. M. Chisholm's evaluation of Sextus Empiricus.

'His most significant contributions are: first, the positivistic and behavioristic theory of signs which he opposed to the metaphysical theory of the Stoics; secondly, his discussion of phenomenalism and its relation to common sense claims to knowledge; and, thirdly, his account of the controversy over the principle of extensionality in logic where the anticipation of contemporary doctrines is perhaps most remarkable.'[1]

However, we have Sextus's own word that as a sceptic whatever his own interest in the theories and doctrines current in his time, he himself subscribed to none of them. According to Chisholm's assessment, therefore, modern philosophers should be indebted to Sextus not for his careful statement of his own sceptical view, but for the detailed account he gives of the philosophical doctrines to which scepticism happened to be exposed at that time and of the arguments with which the sceptic combatted them. Chisholm, however, sees Sextus not only as an expounder of doctrines, but also as a subscriber to them. Thus he attributes to Sextus the thesis that metaphysical objects (God, among others) do not exist 'since we are unable to conceive anything which is non-empirical', and the doctrine that 'indicative signs have no reference' (Chisholm, *ibid*.), as well as claiming that Sextus opposed metaphysical statements on pragmatic grounds—that is, on the grounds that they were apt to engender futile controversy and would interfere with sceptical quietude.[2]

The close connection between twentieth-century empiricism and Sextus's Pyrrhonism is obvious. But it is unfair to portray Sextus as a supporter of any kind of doctrine that we have knowledge only of appearances or of what is immediately given in experience. Phenomena in Sextus's terminology are indeed self-evident, but not in the sense of self-known. For we do not *know* anything simply in so far as something appears.

[1] 'Sextus Empiricus and Modern Empiricism', *Philosophy of Science*, Vol. 8 (1941), p. 371.

[2] Chisholm writes: 'In this context he seems to suggest that metaphysical statements might be true, even though not known to be true, but it is doubtful that he intended this, in view of his doctrine that indicative signs have no reference. He opposed such statements, not merely because he regarded them as nonsense, but also because he believed them to engender futile controversy which seriously interferes with that quietude or ataraxy which is the sceptic's ultimate goal. The objection is primarily a pragmatic one' (*ibid*., p. 375).

Chisholm remarks: 'Although the sceptic does not deny appearances, he does deny the possibility of knowledge which refers beyond them.'[1] It is a main point of Sextus's account, however, to make us understand that he neither denies nor affirms the possibility of knowledge, but lets the question remain open. It is true that Sextus does not deny appearances, in the sense of refusing to accept them; but he neither asserts nor denies *statements* like 'It is hot' or 'I feel hot' or any other statement said to express what appears to him. Appearances are 'beyond question' (Chisholm, *ibid.*), but not in the sense of furnishing or expressing knowledge. If they are beyond question, they are also beyond answer.

6. THE SCEPTIC'S REFERENCE TO THE EXISTENCE OF OPPOSITE VIEWS

Another misconception is that the sceptic's constant references to disagreements are a kind of argument, by appeal to particular cases, for a general conclusion that truth is beyond our grasp. Here we have both a misinterpretation of the sceptic's references to particular arguments, and a miscalculation of his philosophical acumen.

The sceptic does not *expect* to sustain his *isosthenia*, he does not anticipate the outcome of an evaluation for and against, and his appeal to counterarguments is entirely *ad hoc*. Faced with a dogmatist who claims a proposition *p* to be true, the sceptic's move would very often be to throw in the proposition 'Not-*p* is true', and to suggest that the dogmatist defend *p* and attack not-*p*. But if the dogmatist now produces an argument, a pro-argument in relation to *p* or a counterargument in relation to not-*p*, it is natural for the sceptic to throw in what dogmatists with views different from the one he is facing have argued against that very pro-argument or counterargument. The enterprise is always experimental, to set one argument against another, and the origin of the arguments is itself of little importance. To find new, good arguments is no easy matter, and the sceptic cannot be blamed for making a start with those already available to him.

It is therefore natural that in his works Sextus should constantly refer to disagreements between philosophers, listing different, more or less contrasting views on a great variety of subjects. Often he announces when he is leaving arguments found among

[1] *Ibid.*, p. 377.

dogmatists and proceeding to add some that have been invented by sceptics.

Even painstaking students of Greek scepticism misjudge Sextus on this extensive listing of disagreement. Thus Victor Brochard writes:

'It is in its reasoning that scepticism fully reveals its weakness. It is clear, indeed, that there is only one condition on which the impossibility of the human mind's attaining truth could be legitimately inferred from the disagreement of opinions and of systems, namely that this disagreement could only be explained by the fact that there is no truth or that truth is inaccessible to us.'[1]

But there is no inference of the kind 'There is extreme disagreement between holders of opinions and systems, therefore it is impossible for the human mind to reach truth' to be found in Sextus's works. In the first place, the sceptic would not claim truth for either premise or conclusion separately, and secondly, he would not claim validity for the inference from premise to conclusion. Suspension of judgment (cf. stage 4 in the sceptic's genesis) applies here too. If we found evidence of Sextus making the three claims there would of course be reason to invoke the view so popular in accounts of Sextus, that he was not very bright and most likely misrepresented the great sceptics.

As for holding that truth cannot be reached, Sextus mostly refers to the exponents of this view as being non-sceptical, and non-dogmatic: they are what he calls the Academicians. With respect to a truth claim that 'Truth cannot be reached', Sextus would, if our summary is correct, suspend his judgment. 'Truth cannot be reached' is not even one of the (standard) sceptical phrases; it seems, then, that it is not to be used as expressive of the sceptic's mind during his encounters with dogmatists.

But in any case Brochard's implicit view regarding the purpose of the selection of material referred to or quoted in the works of Sextus is a misrepresentation. The sceptic quite simply does not use disagreement as an argument for scepticism. He is much more tentative and judicious. He amasses arguments in the course of a

---

[1] V. Brochard, *Les Sceptiques grecs* (F. Alcan, Paris, 1887), p. 395. 'C'est dans le raisonnement que le scepticisme montre toute sa faiblesse. Il est clair, en effet, que du désaccord des opinions et des systèmes on ne pourra conclure légitimement à l'impossibilité, pour l'esprit humain, d'atteindre la vérité qu'à une condition, c'est que ce désaccord ne puisse s'expliquer que s'il n'y a pas de vérité ou si elle nous est inaccessible.'

perilous career. Although his counterarguments therefore naturally tend to consist of already existing arguments, and in this
sense he makes use of disagreements, he does not appeal to disagreement as such. He tries out counterarguments in concrete
cases: a dogmatist asserts 'p' and the sceptic throws in a 'How
about so-and-so's counterargument "q" against "p"?' Which is
very different from inferring the impossibility of finding truth
from the existence of dogmatists holding 'p', 'not-p', 'q', 'not-q',
and so on.

Incidentally, it is also the failure to grasp the *ad hoc* nature of
radical scepticism that underlies criticism of Sextus as a bad
stylist and expositor. The translator of the Loeb Classical Library
edition of Sextus's works, R. G. Bury, remarks in his introduction
that Sextus 'wearies the reader by his way of piling argument
upon argument for the mere sake of multiplying words—bad
argument and good heaped together indiscriminately'. However,
it must be the uninformed reader Bury refers to, since he himself
gives an excellent account of the character of Sextus's texts,
indicating that they are not intended to be read word for word:

'Obviously his books are not intended to be works of art, but rather
immense arsenals stored with all the weapons of offence and defence
of every conceivable pattern, old and new, that ever were forged on
the anvil of Scepticism by the hammer blows of Eristic dialecticians.
From these storehouses the Sceptic engaged in polemics may choose
his weapon to suit his need; for (as Sextus naïvely observes) the Sceptic
is a "philanthropic" person who spares his adversary by using against
him only the minimum of force necessary to bowl him over, so that the
weakest and most flimsy arguments have their uses as well as the
weightiest.'

This corresponds exactly with the interpretation I am pro-
posing, except that it is difficult to see why Sextus should be considered naïve in his account of the sceptic's manner of arguing.
Not only does it fit in very well with other things he says, but
even today meeting arguments with sufficiently strong, but not
more than sufficiently strong, counterarguments is a sophisticated
procedure. The kinds of arguments used depend on the status of
discussion at the time at which the sceptic throws the argument
into the debate (without participating in it). Therefore a sceptical
manual would need constant revision, new editions coming out
from time to time. But no 'bad' or weak argument should be left
out if it is adequate in a given situation. Accordingly Sextus's

manual should not be read as a Platonic dialogue but as a reference work to be consulted at appropriate moments. As such it is well compiled and efficiently enough organized. Of course the procedure of considering every argument on its own merits is characteristic of all critical philosophy. It is in his continuing and pervasive suspension of judgment that the Pyrrhonist differs from the ordinary critical philosopher. And it is in this apparently wilful refusal to believe or accept anything that those otherwise sympathetic with the Pyrrhonist's procedure have found the absurdity or impossibility of his brand of scepticism. If only this perverse element were removed the critical philosopher would find in the Pyrrhonist a brother in arms. Thus Hume, who denied that there could be 'any such absurd creature . . . who had no opinion or principle concerning any subject', allowed that a moderate scepticism 'may be understood in a very reasonable sense, and is a necessary preparative to the study of philosophy'. But what a distance from the Pyrrhonist in Sextus's account to the methodological sceptic in Hume's who, as Hume goes on to say, 'hopes to reach truth, and attain a proper stability and certainty in [his] determinations'![1]

Russell, too, has favoured a criticism of knowledge that is not 'the attitude of the complete sceptic'. Absolute scepticism is unreasonable; rather it is 'Descartes' "methodical doubt", with which modern philosophy began . . . [that is] the kind of criticism which we are asserting to be the essence of philosophy. His "methodical doubt" consisted in doubting whatever seemed doubtful; in pausing, with each apparent piece of knowledge, to ask himself whether, on reflection, he would feel certain that he really knew it.' Such criticism, thinks Russell, constitutes philosophy. But there is some knowledge, for example, of the existence of our sense-data, which to him appears 'quite indubitable, however calmly and thoroughly we reflect upon it. In regard to such knowledge, philosophical criticism does not require that we should abstain from belief'.[2] We should not reject 'the beliefs which do not appear open to any objections, however closely we examine them'.[3]

Russell's exposition is convincing only so long as he refrains

[1] Hume, *An Enquiry Concerning Human Understanding*, Sect. XII, Pt. I.

[2] *The Problems of Philosophy* (Oxford Paperbacks University Series, Oxford University Press, London, 1967), p. 87.

[3] *Ibid.*, p. 88.

from giving examples of the kind of conclusive knowledge he means, that is, so long as he abstains from applying his principle concretely. However, the various concepts of sense-data are of course highly controversial, and calm and thorough reflection is apt to disclose that any highly conceptualized belief in sense-data is indeed open to objection, especially when made precise in its relation to conceptual frameworks of psychology and epistemology. What Russell establishes is that beliefs which are not open to any existing objections are not open to any objections. Not being objected to, he infers that they are unobjectionable.

Of course, the complete sceptic in Russell's terms cannot be the Pyrrhonist according to Sextus; the Pyrrhonist would not require us to abstain from a belief to which we could find no objection however calmly and thoroughly we reflected. He would simply not allow that he had as yet come across such a belief. Should he do so, of course, his suspension of judgment could no longer be sustained by a balance of arguments, and he could then no longer be a sceptic of the kind described. Being a sceptic of that kind, he could *not* have found a belief immune to objection. As it is, the example given by Russell of such a belief is hardly likely to strike him as a very likely specimen.

The continuation of Russell's account, on the other hand, could safely be acquiesced in by the Pyrrhonist.

'The criticism aimed at, in a word, is not that which, without reason, determines to reject, but that which considers each piece of apparent knowledge on its merits, and retains whatever still appears to be knowledge when this consideration is completed.'[1]

If there is nothing left over, nothing will be retained.

7. THE MATURE SCEPTIC, A MODERATELY KEEN SEEKER AND DOUBTER?

If the sceptic's suspension of judgment must be based on his failure as yet to find decisive arguments for or against, the question arises as to how much we should expect of the sceptic in his efforts to overcome this failure. Are there minimum requirements? In cases where the sceptic takes no steps at all to find arguments, might not his failure to be convinced be a matter for reproach? Should we not regard him as a sceptic only by default?

[1] *Ibid.*, p. 88.

Here we must first recall that an essential feature of the sceptic we are describing is his openness of mind. According to stage 7 (see p. 5) he is a seeker, and since this, like the *ad hoc* nature of his scepticism, is a matter of definition, it is acknowledged that we are in any case concerned with someone who shows a degree of interest. Consequently our sceptic cannot be accused of evading the issues. He may not be continually racking his brains for arguments—as indeed is unlikely in the case of one who does not expect to find the truth—but he must at least be open to argument and even to conviction. Arguments always interest him, and if he is someone who does not expect to find the truth, this is only because past disappointment has destroyed his previous optimism about finding it. It is no part of the definition of the sceptic that he is constitutionally either unprepared to face arguments or impervious to their force.

The question remains as to whether openness itself is enough. The normal view is probably that it is not, for the sceptic is normally conceived as a doubter. Indeed, it is thought a valid objection to scepticism that one *cannot* persistently doubt all that the sceptic doubts. To be a sceptic, according to this view, is necessarily to be in a perpetual state of indecision; a moment's confidence or certainty is enough to burst the fragile bubble, to disqualify one as a sceptic.

But there is no reason why we should think of the sceptic in this way, as one who should, ideally, hesitate before every step to question whether the assumptions on which it is based are valid. Indeed, before raising such a question the sceptic would want to know what the assumptions were, or whether there were any, and what was meant by 'assumption' in this case; and in so far as answers to such questions involve explicit and more or less complicated conceptualizations, all of this would go beyond what the sceptic felt he had any settled opinion on. Any display of confidence, as far as he is concerned, may or may not be a matter of assumptions. At least it is not obvious that the sceptic must avoid all trust and confidence, or that his behaviour must be characterized by doubt and indecision. Perhaps, as we shall see in the next chapter, there is no real call to consider the sceptic a doubter at all.

There is nothing very important in *terminology* at this point: if one wishes to retain the image of a sceptic as a doubter rather than a truster, this itself will not lead to misconceptions as long as one remembers that in the history of thought the greatest sceptics were also great champions of trust and confidence and of common sense *in action*, however brutal they were in criticizing ordinary thinking in its use of the notions of true or false, valid or invalid. In answer to the question, then, of what, and how much, we should expect of the sceptic, I see no grounds for asking more of him than of dogmatists. A man who adheres to the doctrines of Plato, Spinoza, or Kant, or has a more or less individual outlook of his own, and who makes truth claims or claims of objective validity, is open to criticism if he does not from time to time consider and reconsider arguments against his position. But it would be preposterous to ask him to do this daily, especially if he is not a professional philosopher.

Applying the same norms to the sceptic, one must surely allow that the exercise of suspension of judgment as a mental act need not go so far as to colour the sceptic's private life. There is no need for him every day to consider judgments involving truth claims and come to the result that there is no decisive argument pro or con. Although there will certainly be *occasions* for suspension of judgment, there will be no constant need for it.

Similar considerations apply to the sceptic as a 'seeker'. He is counted a seeker because he has not found truth and he leaves open the possibility of finding it. Nothing is prejudged in the idea of his openness about how eager he should be to find the truth in any definite matter. Indeed, as we suggested, his main non-cognitive motivation for finding truth is no longer there: the peace of mind which he was seeking is already found. There remain cognitive and practical motivations, and the strength of these may vary among different sceptics.

The basic complaint of the Pyrrhonian sceptic against all others (the dogmatists, including the Academicians) is that they are guilty of rashness (haste, recklessness, *propeteia*). They leap precipitately to conclusions about truth, falsity, knowledge, or certainty. As against this, one should *wait* until arguments for are decisively stronger than arguments against, or vice versa. (In order not to be accused of dogmatism, the Pyrrhonist will refrain from claiming the truth or objective validity of any point in the logic of argumentation. He speaks about his own behaviour in discussions in terms of propensities, and the like. Among the examples of rashness Sextus mentions is that of deciding upon the question whether something can be grasped [with certainty] or not [Bk. I, 237]).

Since the sceptical phrases we have mentioned are expressive of the sceptic's state of mind when confronted with dogmatists, it is doubly misleading to say without qualification, as Brochard does, that their function is to 'express his doubt',[1] and to portray the sceptic as being more in doubt than others (at times when he is not confronting a dogmatist).

It is important to distinguish doubting and suspension of judgment. Suspension of judgment is the basic trait of the sceptic when confronted with dogmatic assertions. The question of how much, how often, and in what sense doubt must, or is likely to, accompany or precede the suspension of judgment is an open question. There is no reason at all to postulate a *state of doubting* as a main ingredient, or constantly accompanying characteristic, of the mind of one who suspends judgment. And yet it is just this identification of doubt with suspension of judgment that so often mars references to the Greek sceptics. Not that in the *genesis* of a sceptic, doubt and indecision play no part; indeed, the gifted people in Sextus's narrative were led to scepticism precisely by the disquieting doubt and indecision induced in them by the contradictions in things. And the *ataraxia* which Sextus describes is intended as a means of eliminating just that state of disquiet.

8. THE SCEPTIC, A PHILOSOPHER?

For every hundred references in the literature to Academic scepticism (negative dogmatism) there is scarcely one to Pyrrhonism as described by Sextus. And of the many references to Pyrrho and Sextus, few do not hint at negative dogmatism.

One main reason for this is an apriorism and universalism that has deep roots in nearly all philosophical literature. Because 'the sceptic' does not state *a priori* that knowledge *cannot* be reached, that knowledge is impossible, or because he does not adduce arguments against the possibility of knowledge in general, but only throws in particular arguments against particular knowledge claims, he is not counted a real philosopher; instead he is summarily referred to the psychologists and psychiatrists. Because he does not meet them on their own battlefield—apriorism and universalism—real philosophers are not supposed to worry about him.

To be fair, the philosophers have a stronger point: the sceptic

[1] *Les Sceptiques grecs*, p. 332.

of the pure Pyrrhonist community ventures *no proposition whatsoever* that includes a truth or probability claim. And surely a person who is propositionally mute places himself outside the philosophical community. Or does he?

If a sceptic has developed his suspension of judgment and has thrown in arguments against all the philosophical doctrines of his time, the philosophers may still refuse to take his scepticism seriously simply because the sceptic does not claim that he will continue to retain his attitude. Scepticism seems to be *ad hoc*, provisional, transient, or even spasmodic.

There are two answers to this. First, adherence to any doctrine is liable to lapse. However certain a Spinozist or Neothomist may be that he will never alter his views, a change is not precluded. The sceptic, of course, declares nothing, but why should this make a change more probable in his case? Nor need the *ad hoc* nature of scepticism affect the matter—the mature sceptic says no more than that *up to now* he has not been brought out of his *epoché*, but that this might well occur at some time in the future. The fact that the sceptic is more willing than most to acknowledge the possibility of his own defection does not make this event more likely in his case than in that of others. Secondly, scepticism does not really deserve to be called provisional, transient, or spasmodic, because there is nothing in it that conceptually supports these characteristics; and when we come down to considering views in terms of the actual behaviour of their exponents and adherents, we find that any bent of mind may spend itself or wither and any doctrine be abandoned or transcended.

Certainly the sceptic does not and cannot *participate* in the philosophical debate. There is no argument which is *specifically* antisceptical. When the sceptic throws an argument into a philosophical debate, and a philosopher finds it worth consideration, the sceptic may support it or fight it with a set of arguments. In doing so, however, he argues neither for nor against a sceptical position. But if he tends towards *isosthenia*, his development may well continue in the way described by Sextus, and he may end up as a mature sceptic (in our terminology).

As to whether scepticism counts as philosophy, if we accept as a necessary condition for anything to be philosophy that it must contain at least one proposition, or at least one doctrine, claimed to be true or probable, then scepticism is *not a philosophy*. The question is largely terminological, but even if we adopted this not at all traditional way of speaking there would still be room for calling scepticism a basic philosophic attitude or an existential-philosophy (with a hyphen!), and the sceptic a (genuine) philosopher.

Philosophical tradition embraces many philosophers whose 'philosophy' contained not a single proposition with a truth claim, or at least whose programme or intention was of that character. From and including Socrates there have been propositionally innocent philosophers through all periods up until the logical empiricists and various Anglo-American movements inspired by Wittgenstein. It is a commonplace in various quarters that philosophy is really a kind of activity, for example, that of clarifying meanings. And although logical empiricists mingled with scientists, they insisted that as philosophers it was not up to them to take a stand for or against propositions in the non-formal sciences. While the formal sciences for their part were so conceived as not to contain any propositions.

But terminology may not, after all, be very important at this point, and so long as we may call scepticism a philosophical attitude, or existential-philosophy, and its articulate representatives philosophers, I shall not insist that scepticism be called a philosophy. Perhaps 'an ingredient of a philosophy' would be an apt description, since the genetic definition may be satisfied by persons showing deep differences in outlook and basic attitudes. A number of primitivisms, anti- or ir-rationalisms are compatible. And because the sceptic has intimate relations with a *particular* culture and tradition, deep cultural differences will affect him. There will not be an international or intercultural brand of sceptics as there might be of, say, rationalists.

From this, incidentally, it should be clear that there can be no psychology *of* the various sceptical philosophies, if by 'psychology' one means a scientific discipline. The definitions of the phenomena to be investigated by such a psychology would reflect the differences in philosophy.[1] And the sceptic listening to these definitions or delimitations of psychology and the norms stipu-

---

[1] Consider, for example, how a scepticism with phenomenological colouring might develop. It might start with the doctrine of *Wesensschau* and of *Evidence* as applied to the principle of contradiction. Concentrating on the very phenomena of truth and knowledge as possibilities, *Wesensschau* might lead to a rejection of the applicability of the distinction between 'being the case' and 'knowing *p* to be the case'—especially '*one* knowing *p* to be the case'—and 'not being the case', etc., to the deliverances of *Wesensschau*.

lated or announced in its methodology would want to know whether truth or knowledge was claimed. If not, he would suspect he had met some colleagues. Otherwise he would presumably throw in a counterargument. Every definite set of assumptions made by psychologists would be contested by the sceptic, and therefore also every psychological conclusion about scepticism.

One of the most intriguing peculiarities of the sceptic is his constant use of the distinction between true and false, or, better, the distinction between something being the case and not being the case. He compares *pro*-arguments with *contra*-arguments and announces that he does not think they are *strong enough* to establish the truth or superior probability of a doctrine (or its negation). In doing so he implies a belief or conviction that the distinction between true and false is relevant and worth using. At least from the dogmatist's point of view the sceptic appears as a perfectionist, a person with an unusually high requirement of evidence purporting to establish truth, and a tendency to extend the realm or field of application of the distinction between true and false. For where most philosophers would tend to talk in terms of suppositions, assumptions, rules, and stipulations, the sceptic asks, Do these sentences express *truths*?

It is pertinent to ask, therefore, whether the sceptic has ever questioned his own at least implicit acceptance of this distinction. The mature sceptic sees how in everyday life people use 'I know that p', 'p is perfectly certain', 'I cannot be mistaken' in a very loose fashion, with an extremely low standard of evidence compared to that required, for example, in geometry. He himself is also a great exponent of loose talk in so far as he is conceptually unpretentious and without any definite conceptual framework. Why, then, does he apparently not join in the loose use of the terms 'true', 'certain', 'real', and 'known'?

It must be that his development has somehow made these terms stand out separately from the rest. Because of this he can honestly say that as a mature sceptic he is 'still seeking'. For he has retained conceptualizations of 'true', 'certain', 'real', 'known' which permit him to suspend judgment in cases in which everyday uses of the terms would force him to exclaim 'This is true!', 'This is perfectly certain!', 'This is how the thing really is!', 'That I know!'

Suppose, however, that a sceptic were to give up these remaining conceptualizations of the seeker, the zetetic; what kind of philosophy would one get then? The sceptic, it seems, would cease to be a sceptic and come close to being a later Wittgensteinian, at least according to one main interpretation of the latter's *Philosophical Investigations.*

According to that interpretation there already exists a definite 'logic' of the terms 'true' and 'known', and this logic is such that there are a great many things we know perfectly well; for the language we use does not provide room for meaningful doubt here. Moreover, a science of language, a conceptualized doctrine *about* the logic of these terms, is not needed because the pertinent facts can be shown, pointed to. Because philosophy leaves everything as it is, its conceptualizations, *including* the distinctions between true and false and between known and unknown, cannot result in any change in the logic of the everyday use of the terms it has borrowed.

As regards what evidence we require in order to know, there is a term 'conclusive evidence' which also has its own logic of use. This can be shown by asking, *When* is it *legitimate* to say 'This evidence is conclusive'? The question 'Is evidence ever conclusive?' cannot be raised. The distinction between conclusive and non-conclusive is already built into the language and this implies that there is a proper use of 'conclusive' as well as of 'inconclusive'. So if someone were to come and say that in every case in which 'conclusive' has been used, 'inconclusive' was the appropriate term, he would clearly violate the existing logic of the distinction.

Thus the mature sceptic is only a partial conformist, he inevitably encounters opposition when responding sceptically to requests to subscribe to the absolutes of his community—the proclaimed truths, the propositions everyone must *know to be true.* The Wittgensteinian in the above interpretation, on the other hand, is an enlightened, but total, conformist. Even when it comes to the basic zetetic terms, he asks, What is it *legitimate* to say? What am I *justified* in saying? What are the standards of *the community* in assessing evidence? What is *socially* acceptable as conclusive evidence?

Although the mature sceptic does not participate in the philosophic debate, we have seen that he nevertheless throws arguments into it; nor does he rule out the possibility that eventually he will become a participant—if a dogmatist can convince him of the truth of at least one proposition. In any case he accepts the

SEXTUS EMPIRICUS

concepts and arguments of dogmatists as meaningful and all their views as possible views. Although the Wittgensteinian portrayed above resembles the mature sceptic in not participating in the debate, in all other respects the difference is profound: the Wittgensteinian does not throw in arguments, and he definitely rules out the possibility of active participation. Nor does he accept the concepts and arguments of dogmatists as meaningful, and he rejects the possibility of their views being true doctrines.

9. DEFINING SCEPTICISM

In this chapter we have tried to clarify certain distinctions made by Sextus which are vital to a grasp of the significance of Pyrrhonism as a philosophy or a philosophical attitude. These distinctions, between Academic scepticism and Pyrrhonism, between sceptical and dogmatic ways of announcement, and between suspension of judgment and doubt, all play an important part in the credibility of Sextus's portrayal of the sceptic. From the few, but typical, references to Sextus in this chapter, it will be seen how far extant accounts and evaluations are from taking what he says seriously. Perhaps it is the prevailing philosophical preoccupations, now and in the past, that have done Sextus the greatest disservice, by obscuring the value of the distinctions that he is at pains to stress. Consequently Pyrrhonism tends to be regarded as an extreme scepticism, at best an impracticable ideal, and to be classified along with other less radical, but supposedly more possible, forms under definitions that take little account of what Sextus actually wrote. This is true even of R. H. Popkin's formulations of scepticism in his excellent contribution to the *Encyclopedia of Philosophy*. Popkin opens, as is traditional in encyclopedias, with a vague formulation suggesting some kind of definition: 'Skepticism, as a critical philosophical attitude, questions the reliability of the knowledge claims made by philosophers and others.'[1] But such a formulation fails to do justice to Pyrrhonism. Pyrrhonism is not an attitude of epistemological questioning alone; an adequate conception of the kind of questioning it is must take account of the distinctions we have mentioned as well as such aspects as *ataraxia* and trust.

Popkin's next, more precise, formulation, that philosophical

[1] 'Skepticism', *The Encyclopedia of Philosophy* (Collier-Macmillan, London, 1967), Vol. 7, p. 449.

sceptics 'have questioned whether any necessary or indubitable information can actually be gained about the real nature of things' (*ibid.*), though applicable to Pyrrhonism and some other forms of scepticism, applies equally to any philosophy that criticizes necessity and indubitability or concepts of real nature. Carneades, on the other hand, was a sceptic who, although he questioned necessity, and perhaps also indubitability, seems to have believed in differences in probability. It is clear—and of course Popkin does not deny this—that the appraisals and arguments appropriate to probabilists differ greatly from those that apply to Pyrrhonian scepticism.

Popkin continues: 'Skeptics have organized their questioning into systematic sets of arguments aimed at raising doubts' (*ibid.*). But for the Pyrrhonian sceptic, as a seeker after truth, it would be inappropriate to mention a specific aim of any kind, except perhaps as just one of a cluster of aims. It is true that the mature sceptic tends to influence the dogmatist in the direction of scepticism, and this may take the form of inducing him to doubt; however, in doing so he is only following his so-called natural impulses of sympathy, as Sextus would say in his capacity of metasceptic. As for his own future, the mature sceptic is naturally on the lookout for decisive arguments that might bring his scepticism to an end. But here the *listing* of arguments, if it can be said to have an aim at all, should strictly speaking be regarded as having the heuristic aim of eliciting new and better arguments through which to preserve his *ataraxia*.

Finally, in formulating a notion of extreme scepticism, Popkin says that: 'Extreme skepticism questions all knowledge claims that go beyond immediate experience, except perhaps those of logic and mathematics' (*ibid.*). Sextus and others, however, have questioned even logic and mathematics. And if my previous analyses are adequate, the Pyrrhonian questions all knowledge claims, including those which, in a more recent terminology, may be called 'knowledge claims that do *not* go beyond immediate experience'. The Pyrrhonist 'acquiesces in the appearances' not because of any truth or adequate cognitive status that he attaches to the 'angelic' messages which convey the appearances but because such messages convey no knowledge claim at all. A scepticism that contains knowledge claims of or about immediate experience is not an extreme scepticism, at least along one dimension of comparison. But of course a main difficulty in the way of any attempt to delimit an extreme scepticism is the low degree of comparability of extremes of scepticism along the different dimensions that we referred to at the beginning of the chapter.[1] A scepticism that makes no positive claims at all might, for example, be thought to be less intense than one that denied the possibility of knowledge beyond immediate experience, for at least the former scepticism allows for a possibility that the other rejects. Perhaps the word 'extreme' is best avoided; it would certainly be very misleading to describe the Pyrrhonist himself as an extremist of any kind. It might be appropriate, on the other hand, to regard him as a radical, for his scepticism, if not extreme, is extremely thorough and consistent.

[1] See pp. 2–3 above.

II

THE PSYCHOLOGICAL
POSSIBILITY OF SCEPTICISM

I. INTRODUCTION

ONE of the most common objections levelled against scepticism is that however consistent it is in itself, it cannot be serious. Sceptical doubts are not real doubts but only theoretical. Furthermore, it would be impossible to put sceptical theory into practice, for to be consistently sceptical, so it is held, would be to sentence oneself to a life of inactivity; as soon as one begins to do something one begins to take certain things for granted, to believe in them and hence not to doubt them.

The assumption that scepticism, though rational, is patently untenable is fairly widespread. It is voiced, for example, by A. J. Ayer in *The Problem of Knowledge* when he writes: 'No doubt we do know what [the sceptic] says we cannot know, we are at least called upon to explain how it is possible that we should.'[1] This quotation sets the pattern for much of the current discussion of scepticism. As we shall have occasion to remark again, the problem of knowledge has become the problem of explaining, in the face of the so-called sceptic's arguments to the contrary, how knowledge, as we all no doubt correctly assume, is possible. In other words, scepticism is identified with an argument to be rebutted if we are to justify our claims to know anything at all. The sceptic is a good logician, but somewhere or other there must be a flaw in his argument, either in the process of reasoning or in his premises. For what could be more obvious than that there are at least some statements that we know to be true? And what could be a more obvious demonstration of the sceptic's *de facto* acceptance of this fact than his actual linguistic and non-linguistic behaviour?

[1] A. J. Ayer, *The Problem of Knowledge* (Penguin Books, London, 1956), p. 78.

2. IS SCEPTICISM MORE LOGICALLY THAN PSYCHOLOGICALLY IMPECCABLE?

Some contemporary philosophers put this objection by saying that (what they call) scepticism, though logically consistent, is psychologically impossible: a person can pretend to be, but cannot really be, a consistent sceptic. The most famous exponent of this view, Bertrand Russell, has himself been intimately and personally engaged in questions of scepticism. He puts the matter thus: 'Scepticism, while logically impeccable, is psychologically impossible, and there is an element of frivolous insincerity in any philosophy which pretends to accept it.'[1]

However, Russell, in line with most recent discussions of scepticism, is thinking here not of the sceptical way of Pyrrho, as outlined by Sextus, but of a narrow and much less radical trend of sceptical thinking which he terms 'sceptical solipsism'.[2] Russell finds that it is psychologically impossible in practice to doubt the existence of other minds and of the external world. But in coming to this conclusion he applies concepts of 'other minds' and 'external world' which presume a dualism of a particular and not altogether uncontroversial kind.[3] The Pyrrhonist, however, is not bound to join issue on the question of the existence of other minds or of the external world as conceived by Russell, in so far as these concepts presume a dualism that he sceptically declines

---

[1] *Human Knowledge: Its Scope and Limits* (George Allen & Unwin, London, 1948), p. 9. Cf. also p. 196.

[2] *Ibid.*, p. 191. Russell distinguishes sceptical solipsism, the view that 'there is not known to be anything beyond data' from dogmatic solipsism, the view that 'there is nothing beyond data', although according to Sextus both views should be distinguished from scepticism. Russell's tendency to equate scepticism with the view that knowledge of something or other does not exist or is impossible leads him to quite astonishing assertions. Thus, in a discussion of Pyrrho he states that sceptics 'of course, deny that they assert the impossibility of knowledge dogmatically, but their denials are not very convincing' (*A History of Western Philosophy* [George Allen & Unwin, London, 1945], p. 234). Russell does not say why he finds the denials unconvincing. But surely, if all Sextus's efforts to use ways of announcement compatible with his rejection of negative dogmatism, and all his efforts to show that he could not possibly take the sceptical phrases ('Nothing is known', etc.) as true, are to be registered by the critical historian as mere 'camouflage', the most surprising results might be expected from other philosophical sources. Maybe, in his heart, Plotinus was a follower of Democritus?

[3] In *Our Knowledge of the External World as a Field of Scientific Method in Philosophy* (George Allen & Unwin, London 1914) and later, in various epistemological and ontological works, Russell has tried to develop philosophically satisfactory solutions of problems which many have considered to be pseudo-problems.

either to accept or reject. If he says 'The stone is hot', he will not, in the normal course of events, implicitly distinguish between an inner and an external world and on the basis of this distinction locate the stone's heat either in the external world, as opposed to, say, consciousness, or in an inner mental world completely separate from the external. If led into a discussion about whether the heat really resides in the stone or in the mind, he remains unperturbed, declining to offer judgment. It must be remembered that the most important effect of the sceptic's *epoché* is to preserve him from philosophical discussion. Such discussion, to be technically satisfactory, must be relative to certain conceptual frames, that is, to systems of definitions involving clear-cut distinctions and rules for interpreting the key terms, and these must be adopted in order to get a discussion *pro et contra* going. By maintaining an *epoché* in relation to conceptual frameworks, the sceptic simply refuses to get going.

Sextus's picture of the sceptic is thus quite different from Russell's, in so far as the Russellian sceptic is apparently unable to let himself *trust*, and have confidence in, a crude everyday realism into which such sophisticated problems as these do not intrude. Such trust and confidence at the philosophically uncommitted level is of course precisely what we would expect from the Pyrrhonian sceptic; at least if we are to take Sextus seriously when he characterizes the 'loose' ways of talking employed by the sceptic in expressing his mind undogmatically (cf. Chap. 1, p. 10, above).

The formula 'Scepticism is logically impeccable but psychologically impossible' therefore fails to do justice to the strengths and weaknesses of Pyrrhonian scepticism. Indeed, if the foregoing exposition and interpretation are correct, we should be entitled to adopt a very different formula: 'Scepticism is psychologically impeccable and logically invulnerable.'

The thesis that scepticism is impeccable psychologically, in other words, that it is psychologically possible, perhaps even in some cases desirable, to be a sceptic, may seem harder to defend than the thesis that it is logically invulnerable. To be susceptible to charges of inconsistency scepticism would have to include at least two contradictory propositions; but as we have seen it includes no propositions at all. Scepticism is, therefore, not only not inconsistent but not consistent either. However, the question of inconsistency is not so easily disposed of since, as we shall see, the criticism that scepticism is psychologically impossible in part depends on the supposed objection that whatever the sceptic may or may not say, his actions betray implicit allegiance to beliefs and assumptions, in short, falsify the description of him as a person who suspends judgment on all things.

3. DO THE SCEPTIC'S ACTIONS BETRAY HIS DOGMATISM?

It is objected to scepticism that by persistently withholding judgment the sceptic is flying in the face of his own experience and practice. The basis of the objection is that any display of acquiescence or confidence on the part of the sceptic is tantamount to his acceptance of some proposition.

Thus, for example, the mere fact that I stride confidently into a room might, in most circumstances, be said to be tantamount to accepting the proposition 'This floor will bear my weight',[1] just as the mere fact that quickly withdrawing my foot after ominous creakings might be regarded as tantamount to my rejection of the proposition, and setting each foot down tentatively and with great hesitation tantamount to my withholding it.[2]

According to this assumption, the Pyrrhonist's behaviour would be the measure of his ability to remain a sceptic. Despite his failure to make positive or negative assertions, therefore, there would still be a basis for attributing inconsistency to him; for his actions would imply propositions and the manner of his actions would determine his epistemic attitude towards the propositions. If not necessarily inconsistent, the sceptic would remain sceptical only so long as he remained hesitant. And the world and human nature being what they are, he would be prone to such frequent lapses into dogmatism that to describe him as generally sceptical rather than dogmatic would be misleading, to say the least.

This argument might be given stronger forms. To act at all, it might be said, involves some belief or other; and no matter how diffidently one behaves one cannot act consciously without implicitly accepting the truth, at least temporarily, of some propo-

[1] In some circumstances, of course, it might be more appropriately thought of as tantamount to acceptance of some other proposition, for example, 'This is how a confident man walks into a room'. But the view would be that some proposition or other is implied, and perhaps that enough information about the circumstances would determine which.

[2] The terminology here is that of R. M. Chisholm in, e.g., *Theory of Knowledge* (Prentice-Hall, Englewood Cliffs, N. J., 1966). See especially Chap. 1.

sitions. For example, whatever one's reservations concerning the strength of the floor, one accepts that one has such reservations, that if and when they are borne out one will tend to move downwards rather than upwards, and that if one intended to achieve something by setting foot on the floor, other than, say, merely testing its strength, then this cannot be achieved exactly in the way one was hoping it might. According to this stronger objection, the consistent Pyrrhonist would be resigned to a life of complete inactivity. There might, however, be an even stronger form of the argument, in which it was claimed that the very act of contemplating oneself and one's own inactivity would require implicit acceptance of propositions. If the argument was sustained, the sceptic, so long as he was conscious, could never free himself from a fundamental dogmatism.

What is the relation between acquiescence and confidence, on the one hand, and the acceptance or rejection of propositions on the other? Let us take up this question by considering the relation between action and belief.

If a person claimed to hold certain moral beliefs, for example, and made no moves to act in conformity with them in situations where the beliefs were clearly applicable, his claim would be justifiably disputed. And if a navigator claimed to believe that the earth was flat and continued to employ calculations and instruments whose effective use he acknowledged to depend on the assumption that the world was round, he would be justifiably suspected of being less than honest about what he believed. Thus it does seem that a person's behaviour can tend to show that he does not have certain beliefs he professes to have. Moreover, with beliefs implying some fairly specific patterns of behaviour, as some beliefs surely do, the absence of action falling into such patterns will, saving exceptional circumstances, not only tend to show but conclusively reveal the absence of the corresponding beliefs. Some, like Gilbert Ryle, would assert that believing is never merely 'propositional' but to be prone to *do* certain things; just as believing that the ice is dangerously thin is never only a matter of telling oneself and others that it is so, or of acquiescing in the assertions of others to that effect, but also 'to be prone to skate warily, to dwell in imagination on possible disasters and to warn other skaters'.[1] If pronenesses, too, are to be understood behaviourally the matter is settled, but even without that we can say

[1] Gilbert Ryle, *The Concept of Mind* (Hutchinson, London, 1949), p. 135.

that if to believe something is at least in part to be *disposed* to do this rather than that, then lacking the relevant dispositions one would not have the belief.

The question now is whether it also follows that if one does not have the belief one cannot act in the way of a person who does. For if it does follow then it seems that the sceptic is debarred from all behaviour that can be construed in terms of beliefs and their corresponding dispositions. What William James said of religious belief would apply to all meaningful activity. James stated that 'since belief is measured by action, he who forbids us to believe religion to be true, necessarily also forbids us to act as we should if we did believe it to be true'.[1] If this were to be applied generally, not to believe in the truth of something would be to deny oneself the chance to engage in whatever actions were consequent upon the belief in its truth.

There is one kind of context where one may be said to act in the way of one who has a certain belief which in fact one does not have, and that is the case where one pretends to have the belief. Here acting in the relevant way is not merely allowed but, one would suppose, positively required. However, the sceptic can hardly be let off on the supposition that he is pretending to hold beliefs. Generally speaking, his actions must be seen to arise from genuine dispositions, pronenesses, and so on. In pretending to have a belief, on the other hand, it is precisely the absence of the relevant dispositions that the behaviour appropriate to them is supposed to hide. What we need to ask, therefore, is whether it is possible to have the dispositions to act in certain ways, yet without having the relevant beliefs.

The notion of experimentation may help us here. Why should one not be able, for example, to try out beliefs, much as one tries on clothes? And try them out to the extent of 'putting on' the appropriate dispositions? The experimentation, while it lasted, could be indistinguishable, at least externally, from actual commitment to the beliefs; and the experimenter himself might even become, temporarily, another kind of person, finding himself talking and acting in different and not always premeditated ways; but ways which, planned or not, he would nevertheless say he was not committed to and did not 'own'. Thus however much an experiment resembles the real thing, the experimenter himself does not

1 William James, 'The Will to Believe', *Essays in Pragmatism* (Hafner Publishing Co., New York, 1957), p. 108 fn.

lose sight of the experimental nature of the exercise, and the important point is that while experimenting, he is *ex hypothesi* not yet committed, not yet content.

But how far can the sceptic be understood as an experimenter? If we recall our earlier definitions (see pp. 3–6) of the Pyrrhonist, it may seem that he cannot be regarded in this way at all. We said, for instance, that he found no better grounds for accepting the arguments in favour of a doctrine than for accepting those against it. But the experimenter will surely begin his search by selecting the likeliest candidates among the propositions available to him, at the very least preferring some proposition or other to its negation. Thus to act experimentally would seem to require a preference for propositions whose grounds for potential acceptance do seem stronger than those for potential rejection. To accord with this account of the Pyrrhonist's suspension of judgment, then, the required analogy would have to lack any purposive and selective component; in terms of the clothes analogy we would have to compare the Pyrrhonist's assumption of beliefs to a person putting on clothes for amusement and without any serious thought to their style, quality, or general suitability. But this kind of transaction with beliefs could hardly explain the sceptic's continued adaptation to, and confidence in, the world around him.

Sextus, however, defines the sceptic's suspension of judgment as a state of mental rest owing to which he neither denies nor affirms anything,[1] and we said the sceptic (cf. p. 5, above) was one who has so far not found sufficient weight of arguments *pro* or *contra* to justify a *decision* about what is true or even about what is probable. But if he has not yet been able to decide what is probable, surely he must have been equally unable to decide, in the case of any proposition, that it and its negation are *equally* probable? In that case how can the sceptic *find* that the arguments for a proposition are no stronger than those against it?

That Sextus is not inconsistent here becomes clear when one realizes that in finding a balance between arguments for and against, the sceptic is not arriving at some calculation of the respective weight of the arguments he has arraigned for and against a proposition, and on the basis of this calculation justifying his disinclination to offer judgment. It would be as wrong to interpret the Pyrrhonist in this way as it would to say that in failing to

[1] *Outlines*, Bk. I, 10.

find any arguments strong enough to convince him, he is measuring them against some standard which they must conform to before he will accept them. His suspension of judgment is not based on some specifiable shortcoming in the arguments presented to him, by others or by himself; nor is the balance of the arguments something that he works out according to any theory or rule of thumb. The fact that he does not find the arguments for a proposition strong enough to overcome the force of the arguments against it consists in nothing more than the fact that he, personally, is not impelled by them sufficiently to be able to discount the force of the counterarguments. The sceptic refrains from affirming or denying simply because to stand firmly by some proposition or its negation would be to forfeit an option he feels he must retain if he is to preserve his peace of mind. He is the kind of person who if he affirms or denies something opens himself to the very doubts which led him in the first place to favour suspension of judgment. As we remarked earlier, the question of the possibility of scepticism is really no more than the question of the possibility of there being such a person.

Sextus talks of the sceptic as one for whom the balance between *pro* and *contra* is not disturbed (see point 3, p. 4, above). It would seem quite possible for the more inquisitive and venturesome sceptic, willing to take a chance with his scepticism, to prefer one proposition to another, experimentally, without disturbing the balance. The only relevant measure of whether, and how far, a sceptic can do so is the absence, on his part, of compulsion towards one side *at the expense of* the other. The degree to which he can safely experiment with a belief without succumbing to it, and hence forfeiting his option, will be a matter of his personal psychology.

But the main difficulty is that not all a sceptic does can be regarded as experimental. To be able to experiment with a belief one must first have considered it as a possible truth; but what about all those actions that do not correspond to envisaged possibilities, that cannot correspond to beliefs adopted in practice but not in theory, simply because they are not beliefs that are *adopted*? The sceptic who walks into a room may or may not be experimenting with the belief that the floor will support him, but when he turns the doorknob to open the door, or, having got safely to the other side of the room, brushes the sweat from his brow, these or similar actions could not usually be said to correspond to envisaged possibilities. And yet they would have to be before the sceptic could be said to be not willing to stand by the beliefs they imply. Thus the explanation of the sceptic's actions as experimental will not do as a general defence of the possibility of the sceptic's continuing to act as if he believed in certain truths. Whatever the sceptic says, or does not say, his own more or less unconscious acts speak out for themselves and proclaim his beliefs. But then if his actions say what he himself will not say, his silence is wholly gratuitous.

But why should a person's more or less unconscious acts be described in terms of the adoption of beliefs at all? Why should a person's unquestioning behaviour be understood as putting him, so to speak, automatically on one side or other of a contradiction? Indeed, according to some definitions of 'belief' there would be cases where it was illogical to regard believing as 'propositional' at all. Russell, for example, has defined 'belief' as denoting 'a state of mind or body or both in which an animal acts with reference to something not sensibly present'. Explaining further, he says: 'when I go to the station in expectation of finding a train, my action expresses belief. So does the action of a dog excited by the smell of a fox.'[1] Assuming the excitement of the fox to be as non-propositional as any unconscious gesture on the part of the sceptic, why should the sceptic's unconscious actions be considered as tantamount to 'propositional' beliefs when the fox's patently should not? Would it not be as incorrect to charge the sceptic with inconsistency here as it would to accuse the fox of dogmatism?

Such broad definitions of 'belief', however, may be objected to. We might prefer to say that belief is always propositional and that the confident behaviour of beings incapable of formulating propositions should never be described as believing. A man can believe, but a fox cannot; moreover, even if a man always, to some extent, behaves confidently without prior formulation of and taking a stand to propositions, he is able, as the fox is not, to draw the correct consequences from his own behaviour and to see that it does, if not necessarily amount to belief, at least compel acceptance of certain beliefs once the relevant propositions have been formulated. Thus, on entering a room, a man can reflect on the fact that the floor supports him, and though perhaps deny that his confident entry into the room amounted in itself to be-

[1] Bertrand Russell, *Human Knowledge: Its Scope and Limits*, p. 129.

lieving anything, find himself forced to conclude that the proposition that the floor can support him is true. But why stop here? If the events in one's life compel acceptance of successions of propositions, must not one's unquestioning reliance on innumerable everyday details be itself explained by this continual cancelling of licences to hold options on pairs of contradictory statements? Surely, our unconscious confidence and trust are a kind of summing up of our successes, and based on acceptance of certain general propositions, for example, the proposition that everyday details can mostly be relied upon, or that only in exceptional and usually easily identifiable cases floors are not to be relied upon.

If there was no sense in which the sceptic could acknowledge the reliability of things, either to himself or to others, it would indeed be hard to defend him. If he must always find it inappropriate to say things like 'It held!', 'Of course I didn't think it might give way', then we should want to know why he continued to behave as if he did find things reliable. If his silence is to be more than 'official', we should probably regard it as pathological, as a fear of *saying* anything, rather than an expression of anything approximating to a genuine sceptical attitude.

However, if Sextus is right the Pyrrhonist is not at all barred from acknowledging the appearances, either to himself or to others; he, like everyone else, may utter expressions appropriate to the appearances when the situation calls for him to do so. Sextus, we recall, distinguishes between affirming the truth of what one says and merely acquiescing in the appearances. By making provision for the possibility of a kind of verbal assent to appearances Sextus would allow that the sceptic may convey in words what *appears* to him, but in a way that does not amount to an assertion in the sense in which to assert something is positively to take a stand, as we have said, on one side or other of a contradiction (cf. p. 8, above). Thus, if something feels cold to me and I say 'It feels cold', I may be doing no more than publicizing the appearance; ideally my words are then simple effects of my states of perception, unprocessed by interpretation and conceptualization (including any conceptualization to the effect that this is all they are). I may say 'It seems cold' and yet perfectly consistently neither affirm nor deny the *proposition* 'It seems cold'. Similarly with utterances like 'I wouldn't walk on the floor unless I thought it would hold me'; it may be quite consistent to regard these utterances as appropriate to the occasion and yet deny that the act of walking on the floor either implied or compelled acceptance of the *proposition that* the floor was able to support one's weight.

A sceptic, according to the kind of distinction Sextus indicates, may acquiesce, at the time or retrospectively, in his normal and unimpeded entry into the room; he might even publicize it in the form of a running commentary, saying things like 'Now I'm walking over the floor, a few creaks there, but everything seems all right. There, I've made it!' But in using these words he is only conveying his impression of what happens; he is no more stating that a series of propositions are true than, when he recalls the events later on, he is entertaining propositions to the effect *that* such events occurred. If the context should call for the latter he might refuse to be drawn and say that as for taking a stand in favour of some proposition to the exclusion of its negation, he feels that in the nature of this special kind of case he would rather not commit himself. To assert that something is true is one thing; to give one's impressions is quite another. In the former case one makes use of clear-cut distinctions and concepts, some of which, as will appear in Chap. IV, are awkward, even impossible, to put into practice at all, while the latter is no more than, as it were, letting the events speak for themselves—a case in which the speaker functions 'angelically', as no more than a messenger of the appearances.

The substance of the sympathetic metasceptic's case can be summed up as follows. Confident behaviour, including verbal behaviour, is one kind of event among others. But just as verbal expressions of confidence are not necessarily expressions of statements to the effect that one is confident, so confident action in the world is not implicitly a matter of affirming that something is the case. Consequently, in refraining from taking a stand retrospectively on his own confident behaviour and successes, the sceptic is not prevented from giving retrospective expression to his confidence; retrospective expressions of confidence are no different from any others and there is as little basis in them as in his confident actions generally to support the allegation that he is not a sceptic. His confidence neither implies nor compels in him a commitment to the truth or falsity of propositions.

The strength of the metasceptic's case is suggested by the very difference between acting from impulse and habit, on the one hand, and both formulating propositions and accepting or rejecting them, on the other. They are different activities, if not altogether, at least in degree of complexity and extent of commitment. Moreover, it is impossible to infer one's commitment to the truth or falsity of propositions from observation of one's own behaviour, even verbal behaviour. How would we even go about the task of identifying the supposed propositions on the strength of the behaviour, or locate the concepts in terms of which they are formulated? If it is said that you cannot act without a world in which to act, and that therefore any action on one's part involves the assumption that there is a world, it need only be pointed out that not even on their occurrence on this page do the words 'There is a world' determine a proposition; there is nothing in them to suggest the specific rules of definition and conceptualizations that the sentence they comprise may be used to convey on any particular occasion. As elements in a particular person's behaviour they are as open to interpretation as any other piece of behaviour, and as in the case of non-verbal behaviour, they may not be intended to convey anything 'propositional' at all.

We shall not add more here in support of the metasceptic's case. Later, in Chap. IV, we shall have more to say about the complications involved in asserting truth and falsity. But at least it should be apparent that confident action does not, in any straightforward sense, either involve or compel propositional commitment. If, as Sextus, Hume, James, Russell, and others suggest, nature can make us believe things in the absence of what the intellect would consider good reason for belief in their truth or probability, there would seem, on the contrary, to be some initial plausibility in the view that there is no more than a likelihood on any particular occasion that natural confidence and trust in this or that respect implies a disposition to assert the truth of any corresponding propositions.

4. CAN THE SCEPTIC BELIEVE?

If it is possible to believe a proposition in the absence of intellectually adequate reasons for belief in its truth or probability, is it not also possible to believe it without committing oneself to belief in its truth or probability?

The answer to this question is complicated by a variability in the use of the term 'belief'. Sometimes to believe means to accept that something is certain, sometimes that *one* is certain though *it* may not be, at other times that one is not certain, since one does not *know*, but is only inclined to be certain. As we saw in Russell's definition, 'belief' can even be used to cover behaviour that involves no verbalizable envisaging of states of affairs at all, but simply an attitude of unquestioning expectation. James says that 'there is some believing tendency wherever there is willingness to act . . .'.[1] And he accepts that there is a sense in which 'we find ourselves believing, we hardly know how or why',[2] as if we could come across our own beliefs by observing our own behaviour.

But, then, could not the sceptic also believe what he and others, by noting his actions and words, may find him believing? Certainly, the definition of the sceptic as one who fails to find arguments for or against a proposition sufficiently strong to warrant a decision seems to allow him considerable room for manoeuvre. And the question of whether he can believe or not may only turn on what one chooses to mean by 'belief'. It is clear, for example, that if to believe something he must accept unreservedly some proposition as true or probable, the sceptic cannot believe. If, on the other hand, beliefs are understood more broadly in terms of behaviour which may in principle be dissociated from commitment to the truth or probability of propositions, the sceptic can be a believer. In that case the limits to scepticism may be thought to come where the sceptic's behaviour lends itself more properly to the terminology of 'conviction' rather than 'belief'; in that to be convinced about something suggests a kind of deliberate decision, or at least a decisiveness, that is quite alien to suspension of judgment. However, even this may give the sceptic less latitude than he is due. Is it impossible, for example, to consider an occasion where we could aptly describe, say, participants in a programme of action as having strong convictions about the best way to proceed, and as feeling quite sure that a fair number of envisaged events may be relied upon to occur, and yet deny that they were thereby committed to accepting propositions? At least it could be psychologically incorrect to assume that, if asked, they would seriously maintain that they *knew* what was best, that what they said about the future, for example, the weather, was true. But on what basis, then, could it be claimed that their actions exposed their commitments? Thus we seem to

---

[1] William James, *op. cit.*, p. 89.   [2] *Ibid.* p. 93.

reach a point where, far from any action at all on the part of the sceptic betraying his innate dogmatism, the problem is rather to find any kind of action that could be considered adequate evidence of the kind of commitment that the sceptic, according to Sextus's definition, avoids.

James, we may recall, says that 'since belief is measured by action, he who forbids us to believe religion to be true, necessarily also forbids us to act as we should if we did believe it to be true'. But whether we conclude that here is one kind of activity from which the sceptic is debarred depends on the part we ascribe to commitment in religious belief. James himself argues 'in defence of our right to adopt a believing attitude in religious matters, in spite of the fact that our merely logical intellect may not have been coerced';[1] the abstention from religious belief in the absence of sufficient intellectual justification, he regards as itself an act of will, inspired by the fear of making mistakes. In enjoining us to believe truth rather than shun error in regard to religion, James presupposes that religious belief 'requires, or inspires' certain actions which we would be debarred from if we abstained from such belief. 'The religious hypothesis gives to the world an expression which specifically determines our reactions, and makes them in a large part unlike what they might be on a purely naturalistic scheme of beliefs.'[2]

It is not clear, however, that the sceptic's world cannot be coloured by religious beliefs, and that his reactions cannot be determined by them. The crucial question here concerns the part played in these reactions, and in the expression that determines them, by belief in the truth or probability of religious propositions. We might stretch matters even further and say it concerns the part played in believing in the truth or probability of propositions by *commitment* to their truth or probability. It is true that in some cases membership of a religious community may depend on acceptance of this special kind. On the other hand, it is hard to see what specific reactions membership in this sense could determine, and in any case, communities like these would be just the ones we should expect the sceptic to avoid. Usually, as in the case of political and social ideologies, little pressure is exerted on people actually to affirm the factual truth of whatever religious propositions they subscribe to; it is enough to exhibit an appropriate positive attitude. If there is anything at all that the sceptic

---

[1] William James, *ibid.*, p. 182. [2] *Ibid.*, p. 108 fn.

would seem to be unable to derive from religion, it would be a settled conviction, say, in a personal universe. But even if such conviction plays an important part in religion, it is hardly essential. Conviction and faith, after all, are not the same, and in stressing the difference believers are often insisting upon the sufficiency of the latter.

Our defence of the sceptic may tend to be misconstrued at this point. We may seem to be on the verge of picturing him as being able to participate in the beliefs of his non-sceptical fellow-citizens because his reservations about them concern merely the philosophical status of the evidence available for these beliefs. This kind of defence has often been made on behalf of the sceptic. Popkin, for example, says that 'the historical skeptics . . . distinguished believing various matters from having sufficient reasons for believing them. Regardless of the legends about Pyrrho, the skeptical authors seem to have followed Huet's view that it is one thing to philosophize and another to live, and that many propositions may be philosophically dubious but acceptable or even indubitable as living options.'[1] The reservations of the sceptic thus appear as nothing more than an intellectual appendix attached to everyday beliefs, according to which it is stated that the beliefs in question are philosophically dubious.

However, as we have already pointed out, the Pyrrhonist cannot have philosophical reservations, if by this is meant that he is able to point out with regard to any proposition that the evidence for believing it is philosophically inadequate. As we have stressed, the Pyrrhonist can have no measure of the inadequacy of evidence other than his own continuing reluctance to let the counterarguments go for nothing. And this reluctance is nothing but a personal, not merely philosophical, failure to be convinced. There can be no distinction, in his case, between a living and a philosophical attitude to beliefs.

James defines a living option as one in which both hypotheses make some appeal to one's belief,[2] the extent of this appeal being measured by one's willingness to act. But he distinguishes between the livingness and the genuineness of an option. Although 'Choose between going out with your umbrella or without it' may be a living option in his sense, it is not a genuine one, be-

---

[1] R. H. Popkin, 'Skepticism', *The Encyclopedia of Philosophy* (Collier-Macmillan, London [1967]), Vol. 7, p. 460.
[2] William James, 'The Will to Believe', p. 89.

cause it is not forced; one can avoid going out at all.[1] According to our account the sceptic is a person who finds that no options are genuine in this sense. For, as we have indicated, the sceptic's experience does not formulate *itself* into propositions, nor are the circumstances in which his ordinary everyday expectations are fulfilled or disappointed sufficient in themselves to compel him to take a stand. It is not, as Popkin suggests, that the sceptic relies on a theoretical distinction which makes his reservations about everyday propositions merely formal; but rather that propositions of all kinds involve conceptualizations of experience, and that their acceptance or rejection requires acquiescence in much more than the mere course of events in one's experience.

Russell has an alternative picture of the sceptic acting out a common life with his non-sceptical fellows. He states that 'a modern disciple [of Pyrrho] would go to church on Sundays and perform the correct genuflections, but without any of the religious beliefs that are supposed to inspire these actions'.[2] But this ignores the subtle variations of attitude that the term 'belief' tends to obscure. The sceptic's trust in his own impulses and in the traditions of his environment need not express itself in a mere formal allegiance to the beliefs that his non-sceptical fellow-citizens attach to their actions. The sceptic is not one who, lacking the motive power of any beliefs of his own, must, if he is to move at all, hitch himself to the habits of his society. If he genuflects on Sundays this may be due simply to his having been brought up in a religious household, and having as yet found no compelling reasons to stifle the impulses that the acceptance by others of religious propositions has bequeathed to him. He may still have the appropriate dispositions; being a sceptic he will simply be one who has failed to come to any final decision about the truth of the beliefs from which his actions spring.

But equally the genuflecting sceptic may be a particularly venturesome sceptic, willing to test the power of religious atti-

[1] 'Choose to go out or not to go out' might seem at first sight to be a genuine option, but it is unclear that in subsequently going out or not going out one has necessarily chosen to do so. What if one forgets the option, or goes immediately to sleep, or is swiftly carried out before having decided? Even if one cannot (and perhaps one can) *avoid* the choice, it may elude one. James, however, does not give this as an example of a genuine option. Instead he gives the following example: 'Either accept this truth or go without it.' But, according to our discussion above, even this would be a genuine option only where non-acceptance of the truth could be shown to exclude all ways of participating in it.

[2] Bertrand Russell, *A History of Western Philosophy*, p. 233.

tudes to overwhelm his scepticism. He may even go so far as to acknowledge their power, but still not succumb to them to the extent of excluding the possibility of the relevant religious propositions being false. Here there might seem to be little to distinguish the sceptic from the mature religious believer who strives to sustain his religious attitude on something less than absolute conviction. To the religious minds of Kierkegaard and others, of course, the confusion of knowledge with faith is directly irreligious. On the other hand, one would expect important differences in the attitudes of the religious believer and the experimenting sceptic. The faith of the believer in the truth of religious propositions is something that the sceptic can only pretend to himself that he has; if he really had it he would not be a sceptic. A sceptic's participation in the propositional aspects of religious belief cannot therefore be genuinely religious. But this does not mean that he cannot act and react as he would if he genuinely believed in the truth of the propositions. Moreover, it is debatable how much of the characteristically religious 'expression' which James refers to is dependent on a genuine acceptance of the 'religious hypothesis'.

The difference between impulses and judgment is reflected in our interpersonal relationships. We trust others, some implicitly, others up to a point; and to that extent we may be disposed to make assertions about them which claim truth or probability. But I think that nearly everyone has had occasion to feel that this trust, or mistrust, even if put into words, does not correspond to a definite opinion that, in certain circumstances, we might be required to give, or to any claim to objective validity that we might be called upon to make. Here, too, the sceptic may preserve his naïve attitudes of trust and mistrust, his confidence and diffidence, and the feelings of certainty and of uncertainty that he has for others. His world remains, in this respect, the same as that of the non-sceptic. The only difference is that for him the act of asserting the truth or falsity of a proposition is part of a special occasion in which something quite different is expected of him. Rather than make judgments, he would tend, as Sextus indicates, to cultivate perceptual and emotional sensitivity; and as this sensitivity increased, so would the need for claims of objective truth vanish, or be substantially reduced.

5. MUST THE SCEPTIC BE A DOUBTER?

There are no grounds in Sextus's description for picturing the mature sceptic as a person who shows indetermination, irresoluteness, indecision, wavering, hesitation, suspense, perplexity, bewilderment, embarrassment, confusion, puzzlement, disbelief, incredulity, mistrust, diffidence, or suspicion, however fittingly these terms may describe his state of mind as he listens to dogmatists. But Sextus does list four names of the adherents of his philosophy: the 'sceptics', the 'zetetics', the 'doubters', and the 'Pyrrhonists', and it might seem that of these, the first two deriving from Greek terms for looking about in a searching manner, and particularly that alluding to doubt, suggest characteristics not at all conducive to a profound peace of mind. However, it is clear that Sextus introduces them simply in order to classify abstract philosophies according to how they stand in a particular discussion, namely that on the true knowledge of reality. They need not designate personal traits. There is nothing here to suggest that the sceptic, as an actual person, should feel obliged to go around doubting or seeking any more than others. Indeed, the urge to doubt and seek should apply more to the dogmatist, for, as we have suggested, the more one postulates as true, and the more entangled one gets in the intellectualization of attitudes, the more there is to doubt. By refraining from dogmatizing one may reduce the occasions for doubt. And in any case, the discussion in the two previous sections should have effectively undermined the assumption that the sceptic must be in a perpetual state of doubt and indecision. The sceptic's reservations are simply not of the kind that are directly reflected in his reactions to his surroundings. In so far as they do affect his attitudes and behaviour, these reservations are expressed not in any preoccupation with doubt but in an avoidance of just those dogmatic forms of confidence that tend to give rise to doubt and mental tension.

The difference between the doubter and the sceptic in Sextus's sense can be illustrated by two kinds of dialogues:

The doubter

The dogmatist: *p* is true.
The doubter: I doubt it, there is the following source of error.
The dogmatist: You mean not-*p* is true?

The doubter: I doubt whether not-*p* is true; there is the following source of error. . . .

The sceptic

The dogmatist: *p* is true.

The sceptic: Why should I accept *p* rather than not-*p* as true?

The dogmatist: Because argument *A* proves *p*.

The sceptic: Why should I accept '*A* proves *p*' as true rather than '*B* proves not-*p*'?

Thus, where the doubter is continually disappointed with the candidate convictions that offer themselves for acceptance, the sceptic, resting ('until further notice') in his *epoché*, has no pressing vacancies for them. During his dialogue with the dogmatist there need be no inkling of doubt in his mind.

6. IS THE SCEPTIC UNPERTURBED BY MODERN SCIENCE?

It has been suggested that although scepticism may have been psychologically possible in the Hellenic world, this is only because science at that time played no important role in daily life. Today, however, with scientific knowledge pervading society at all levels, and scientific regularities forming the background of our lives every moment of the day, scepticism can no longer be regarded as psychologically possible.

Although there is much to be said for this point, technical development has also introduced considerable complexity, irregularity, and unpredictability. And of course even in the time of Sextus people relied on the regularities of the seasons, the moon, and the uses of words. Furthermore, even if the beneficiary of modern science has a thousand regularities at his beck and call, unquestioning reliance often invites a rude awakening.

But in any case those who are impressed by scientific methodology will find that truth, as a property of scientific results, has been reinterpreted. This is due to intensive indoctrination with a methodology of science which stresses the uncertainty of scientific knowledge, the commitment to hold any question open and the idea that the main function of scientific propositions is as working hypotheses. Since the dominating philosophies at the time of Sextus —Stoicism, varieties of Platonism, and Epicureanism—were all dogmatic, and the religions of the day claimed to contain true knowledge, our own environment of scientific education and creativity can hardly be considered more hostile to Pyrrhonian scepticism than the environment of Sextus.

In the philosophy of the formal sciences, too, an influential movement stresses postulates, conventions, rules at the base of mathematics, rather than truth and objective validity. The violations are thus conceived as forms of bad, unsocial, or incorrect behaviour.

Uncertainty in natural science does not exclude probability. There are, however, influential movements in philosophy that deny the probability of scientific knowledge. One of them is closely connected with the Catholic Church, representing a variant of Neothomism. Pierre Duhem is an outstanding representative. Another is represented by Karl R. Popper, a great disbeliever in the capacity of induction to justify scientific propositions and of probability as a property given to scientific propositions by their particular confirming instances.

In short, methodology of the sciences, formal and non-formal, is compatible with the view that anything can happen at any time, and that it is unscientific to say that some happenings are *objectively* more probable than others. Our life of action, even in a society pervaded by presuppositions of scientific regularity, is not, of course, dependent upon the correctness of any definite proposition about a regularity. It is enough that we find ourselves *trusting* that the future will resemble the past, or, to be more exact, that we act in a trusting way which may best be suggested by such exclamations as 'Surely the future will resemble the past!', 'You can always rely on the force of gravity!'

So, while many drop from the ranks of potential sceptics because of an unshakeable belief in the truth or objective probabilities of scientific knowledge, others are led to scepticism by their very studies of the special character of scientific knowledge.

7. IS THE SCEPTIC SENSITIVE TO THE DIFFERENCE BETWEEN REAL AND APPARENT?

It has also been suggested that by confining himself to reports of his own beliefs and thoughts the sceptic collapses the distinction between appearance and reality, and thus denies himself the use of the category of the real.

The sceptic, however, does not reject the everyday distinction between what seems to him now to be so-and-so and what really is so-and-so. That is, he may retain a kind of image of the distinction between reality and mere appearance without putting a specific interpretation on it. At least this is how we may understand some of his reactions and utterances. He, just like anyone else, can be misled by illusions, note his mistakes, and correct them. He simply suspends judgment in relation to any proposition claiming to say something *true* about how things really are. To understand the sceptic's mind we must appreciate that reality, in this respect, is utterly in the dark, always eluding him, never grasped in knowledge. But it would be incorrect to picture him as feeling that reality is utterly unintelligible, incomprehensible, unreachable. (That would be the feeling of the Academicians, not of the sceptics, according to Sextus.) Reality is in darkness, but not *necessarily* in darkness; perhaps it can be brought to light; at least he does not know that it cannot. In fact, the sceptic himself may, in his own opinion at least, be the one to bring it to light; he may discover how things really are—in at least one respect. This, of course, would mean the end of his career as a sceptic. But, as was pointed out in Chap. I, it would be wrong to view the sceptic as serving a self-imposed life sentence, or as a person who could not envisage a possible defection to dogmatism.

Tentatively, I conclude that the sceptic contemplating questions like 'How is reality?' and 'What is real?' is likely to feel that reality is *enigmatic, ambiguous, strange, obscure, veiled, unpredictable, unmanageable.* Compared to the dogmatist who thinks he knows a large number of important truths and has full access to a reality that is quite intelligible in most respects, the sceptic is likely to feel more or less powerless. Anything may happen at any moment, there is no certain way of stopping any process, a way that is guaranteed by reality's being regular and understood.

It seems that if a sceptic has a penchant for the contemplation of reality and for wondering about how things really are, he must get depressed or at least awed. I suppose one must acknowledge a need in men for unveiling, controlling, and predicting what is real. On the other hand, of course, there are secondary needs of an opposite kind. Needs for a universe that *is* too great and complex to be understood, a reality which possibly has layers we cannot penetrate, mysterious depths, unfathomable riddles.

So, even if the sceptic is likely to, or will as a rule, feel reality to be enigmatic, ambiguous, and so on, there are, psychologically, different frameworks in which to put these feelings. The resultant complex attitude may quite well not be a negative one of perplexity, fear, embarrassment.

So much for the likely feelings of the sceptic towards reality as opposed to mere appearance, in so far as the distinction is something he acknowledges. One must, however, keep in mind that the fundamental distinction for the sceptic is not that between real and apparent, but between known to be true (or valid) and not known to be true (or valid). The sceptic may ask himself 'Do I really want this gadget?', 'Do I really trust this friend?', because an answer may be found through listening to his own impulses and inclinations, or discriminating between levels or depths of motivation. The sceptic might also say 'The boss looked angry, but he was not *really* angry' without claiming truth, but only by way of conveying his impressions. For there are impressions both of real anger and apparent anger. Thus, in matters of interpersonal relations, the sceptic may, more often even than the dogmatist, consciously discriminate between real and apparent. But he does so without touching epistemological distinctions, or the professional philosophical debate on reality and appearance.

8. GENERAL OUTLOOKS GENERATE SCEPTICISM

The sceptics described by Sextus came to doubt and then suspend judgment through their encounters with dogmatic disagreement and controversy. It may be that today, however, the most likely development of a complete sceptic (surrounded by a dogmatic environment) includes a presceptical stage at which the later sceptic has an intellectually well-organized, unified outlook on life and the cosmos.

From experiments in social and physical perception we know that value-judgments clearly and significantly influence perception. One may remind oneself, for instance, of how coins worth more look bigger. A unified outlook influences all regions of perception. Or, to be more exact, there will be an interaction between different factors and layers of the mind with a resulting personality structure characteristic of the outlook.

The intellectual organization of an outlook inevitably results in a distinction between basic and less basic parts. The mass of

judgments of value and of fact will be felt to rest on certain fundamentals, certain basic assumptions, or intuitive insights.

Having reached this stage the individual is constantly in a
danger zone. If the personality is not highly integrated, but permits the individual with a certain degree of calmness, detachment, or alienation to inspect his own outlook as such, a major
kind of catastrophe or crisis may occur. If, for some motive and
reason or other, inspection is carried out with a touch of basic
doubt or feeling of strangeness, the individual comes to look
upon his own outlook *in its very basic features* as something profoundly subjective, as the truthful expression of one individual
basic way of seeing and feeling things, but without any consequences for any other human being. That is, the holder of an
intellectually well-organized, unified outlook creates some of the
necessary conditions for a thoroughgoing scepticism. He has the
breadth and intensity of vision lacking among people who are
only intermittently and tentatively engaged in working out their
own outlook on life and the cosmos.

From a philosophic, or, let us say, epistemological, point of
view, fundamental principles must have self-evidence, an internal
or immanent obviousness. Being fundamental, they are by
definition impossible to defend by anything external to themselves;
they express a last stand. If, therefore, an individual comes into an
ambiguous relationship to the only foundations he can identify
himself with, the whole edifice that rests on the foundations
becomes suspect. He doubts its truth and validity, yet there is no
objective test available. If his further development goes well, he
will acquire the status of a mature sceptic, enjoying peace of mind.
But he may not develop in this way—he may instead develop
negativism, cynicism, nihilism, despair.

9. CAN WE ASSUME THAT SEXTUS AND HIS LESS ARTICULATE FRIENDS FULFIL THE REQUIREMENTS?

We have, in deference to Sextus, defined scepticism genetically,
in terms of a characteristic personal development. Those and only
those persons who show this development are (by definition)
sceptics.

The possibility of becoming a sceptic is then identical with the
possibility of undergoing this development. And the possibility

of remaining a sceptic is equal to the possibility of continuing to show the characteristics attributed by Sextus to the mature sceptic. Sextus says nothing about persons who do not remain mature sceptics, the 'renegades' or 'backsliders'. These would be sceptics who eventually lose their suspension of judgment in favour of certain propositions—let us say those of Heraclitus or Protagoras.

Although we are not concerned with the question of for how long it is possible or practicable to remain a sceptic, in discussing the psychological possibility of scepticism we nevertheless think of time intervals of some length. A person may scarcely be said to be a Catholic or a Conservative or a pessimist for five minutes— that would be too short. On the other hand, a stability lasting twenty years or more is not required in order to qualify. The same considerations apply to scepticism: there is no built-in requirement of lifelong adherence, but there is, of course, a requirement of stability and profound attachment.

Sextus talks about sceptics as if they were persons existing at and before his time. Very often he uses phrases suggesting that he himself is a sceptic. One must nevertheless pose the question, Was Sextus, or were his friends, *really* sceptics, at least during some part of their lives? Were at least some persons *correctly* subsumable under the concept of sceptic as defined genetically? Or does Sextus only describe ideal sceptics, fictitious personalities?

There is nothing in the writings of Sextus or in other Greek works (for example, those of Diogenes Laertius) which *directly* suggests the fictitiousness of his sceptics. In the literature of his days and earlier, the existence of sceptical 'schools' and sceptical philosophers is taken for granted. More exactly, the term 'sceptical' and its cognates are used to qualify adherents of certain schools and of single personalities.[1]

From a psychological and social point of view, our ultimate decision will mainly build on our assumption as to what is possible *today*. We can try to envisage what might be the difference between human life here and now and life in the Hellenic world, but ultimately the question of the psychological and social possi-

---

[1] On the other hand, the terms do not connote something invariable. Pyrrhonism, as described by Sextus, is, after all, only one kind of sceptical philosophy according to the terminologies using 'sceptical' in more or less broad senses. To take an example, the existence of Carneades and sceptics adhering to his probabilism does not directly support the hypothesis that there also existed Pyrrhonists.

bility of scepticism has to be attacked from our knowledge of the human beings of today.

Concluding tentatively we shall form certain hypotheses:

1. Scepticism is psychologically possible. It is possible in its full development as pictured by Sextus, with the additional features described in the foregoing.

2. Approximation to scepticism is psychologically a more likely and durable state. The same holds good of states in which one's attitudes are too vague or ambiguous in outline to decide upon their exact relations to sceptical requirements.

3. People most likely to develop close approximations to scepticism are those who have a marked tendency and ability to form integrated, general attitudes, colouring their whole mental life and outlook. Such persons will eventually also be able to suspend complex attitudes in the sense of holding them back from full, free operation. The psychological mechanisms behind truth claims and claims of objective validity may thus be suspended.

4. Experience furnishes some material relevant to the situation of a sceptic in a non-sceptical milieu. The conservatism and other social traits of the sceptic are understandable interactions within a dominantly non-sceptical milieu. The possibility of a sceptical 'epidemic', a flourishing scepticism gradually wiping out dogmatism, has never been discussed seriously. The main questions raised are, Would inquisitiveness, and therefore science, come to a standstill? Will children be left untaught? This latter eventuality would have disastrous effects upon any civilization known to men.

5. As to the possibility of stable sceptical communities, there is no precedent to learn from. In such a community, if one could ever come to exist, there would be little incentive for the individual to form a general outlook, and he would not be helped to form one by learning to know existing philosophies. If—as has been supposed—one is most likely to form scepticism when doubt undermines a general outlook to which one has given all one's mind, the main source of scepticism will dry up in communities that are going sceptical. Thus, the community will eventually turn antisceptical, restoring the supremacy of dogmatism in some form or another.

III

SCEPTICISM AND POSITIVE MENTAL HEALTH

I. INTRODUCTION

THERE is a further question which the proposal that scepticism is possible in practice immediately gives rise to, and that is the question of whether, and in what respect, scepticism is at all practically desirable. The host of issues associated with this question cannot be discussed here, but before going on to discuss scepticism in the light of more or less purely epistemological considerations, we can at least pause to consider how scepticism stands with regard to an area where the practical issues have already been formulated in comparatively precise terms, and the normative issues more or less, if only implicitly, agreed upon, namely mental health. What I propose to do here, therefore, is subject the radical sceptic to the test of currently accepted criteria of positive mental health.

A practical problem very germane to the issue of scepticism arises here in confronting the Hellenic sceptic with modern teaching on positive mental health. The exponents are many, and seeker though he is, he can hardly fail to notice with some discouragement that the specialists are not of one mind. Therefore, to protect him from an unnecessarily obvious demonstration of the availability of counterarguments, let us confront him with but one representative, Marie Jahoda. Or, to be more exact, let us confront him with the criteria listed in her book *Current Concepts of Positive Mental Health* (Basic Books, New York, 1959).

2. CONFRONTATION WITH SIX CRITERIA OF POSITIVE MENTAL HEALTH

The first major category of criteria refers to the attitudes of an individual towards his own self. However, I do not think much can be said about that kind of criterion because it does not

61

connect in an obvious way with what Sextus is talking about. But the next criterion opens up interesting questions. Can the sceptic be said to display a satisfactory degree of growth, development, or self-actualization? Gordon Allport explains that growth motives 'maintain tension in the interest of distant and often unattainable goals'. By growth motives he refers to 'the hold that ideals gain upon the process of development'.[1] Now, perhaps it is only possible for unattainable or very distant goals to furnish strong motivation if the individual is convinced that certain propositions are unquestionably true and certain goods absolutely or objectively good. As regards distant goals in general, verbalization plays a decisive role, but I think one must concede that belief in a definite truth is hardly a necessary requirement of one's being said to have a distant goal. Gardeners may plant trees for the joy of their grandchildren but without making definite predictions. The sceptic may make evaluations concerning distant matters that he envisages, and the verbalizations may be part of what stimulates him to act consistently through long periods, but he need not use any of these verbalizations to express knowledge. I tentatively conclude that scepticism is not a decisive obstacle to self-actualization. On the positive side, the sceptic has at least one distant goal, to find truth, and one ideal, true knowledge. As metasceptics we shall attribute this to him even if he always suspends judgment when we discuss this point with him.

A. H. Maslow, stressing self-actualization as a criterion of mental health, finds that it is accompanied by a 'genuine desire to help the human race'. Strong and persistent motivation in helping our race in complete generality, or, somewhat less ambitiously, in helping the developing countries or any considerable portion of mankind (without hating the rest), may well require a heavy reliance on abstract thinking and conclusions derived from such thinking. The sceptic, not being able to concede the truth of even quite simple propositions, may not be able to visualize the problem of helping the human race in its totality. If he meets a hungry child, he meets *that* child, not the fifty million hungry children of the same nationality. He would tend to answer Maslow, 'Yes, I

---

[1] This and the following quotations are all from M. Jahoda, *Current Concepts of Positive Mental Health* (Basic Books Inc., New York, 1959), pp. 33–65. The book is a report written for the Joint Commission on Mental Illness and Health. The purpose of it, according to its author, is 'to clarify a variety of efforts to give meaning to this vague notion' of mental health. The qualification 'positive' indicates that one is looking for something more than mere absence of illness.

think I see the terrible importance of what you are saying, but only in moments in which I succeed in believing in the truth of a long list of propositions. However, I see no grounds for accepting them rather than their negations as true'. Any political, social, or ethical creed based on a substructure of articulated unquestioned truths would be without appeal to the mature sceptic. In conclusion, then, we may suggest that the sceptic would receive a low score if positive mental health were judged by desire to help the human race at large. A good lecturer on the subject of helping mankind, however, will illustrate his points by pictures of starving children, or desperate mothers. The sceptic might be motivated to help, immediately and vigorously, on seeing the pictures and listening to the case studies, whereas the ordinary listener would curb his feelings for political, financial, and other reasons which are highly dependent on belief in general truths. In short, the sceptic may well be more fitted to offer spontaneous and wholehearted help. But if Maslow insists that he must have a strong desire to help *mankind* in order to satisfy the criterion, the sceptic will fail.

As a third category of criteria, Jahoda mentions *integration*. At this point, too, Gordon Allport seems to be the psychologist who makes the sceptic appear most unhealthy. He speaks about a unifying philosophy of life as a sign of maturity. And although the metasceptic and diligent observer of the sceptic has ample reasons to accord a unifying philosophy to the sceptic, this does not seem to be enough for Allport. The mature person 'participates and reflects, lives and laughs, according to some embracing philosophy of life developed to his own satisfaction and representing to himself his place in the scheme of things'.

If we think of a philosophy of life as an outlook on *life in general*, and if it is to be developed in contrast to other philosophies of life, the sceptic has no philosophy of life. He has no *doctrinal* philosophy of life, being antisceptically free of belief in particular philosophical systematizations. Therefore, he cannot place himself as an outsider looking at himself and his place in the general scheme of things. He does not believe that he knows of any objective scheme of things. So, Gordon Allport must conclude, it seems that the sceptic dismally fails, and that he is utterly unhealthy, according to at least one integration criterion.

But there are grounds for the opposite conclusion. About other people we may *say* they have a definite outlook about life, even life in complete intercultural generality, without their saying anything about it either to themselves or to us. We speak about the old peasant's outlook in spite of the fact that one of the old peasant's traits is extreme muteness. He may even protest, swearing that he would never dream of considering life in general, or subject his whole personal life to reflection. Gordon Allport might agree to this. A unifying non-professional philosophy of life may not be articulated in any form. If this is granted, however, the sceptic may rise to a pinnacle of healthiness in so far as he has a way of taking things which is both peculiar and unified.

Our conclusion regarding integration will therefore follow a middle course. One may speak of the sceptic's outlook, and the sceptical way marks an important unifying ingredient. Yet in spite of this he may in many ways show considerable looseness or even disconnectedness: he will conform only roughly to the traditions of his society, according to Sextus. He will perhaps be weak in following principles and norms under stress, not holding them in any absolute manner. He will go along with others, but not all the way, when this requires, as it sometimes will, a solid conviction that this or that *is* true. It is tempting to think of times of crisis, when some, but not all, friends or fellow-citizens stand up to very severe tests. The sceptic's resistance to stress may show weak spots, but not in any glaring fashion. He never makes great claims, his level of aspiration is moderate, and he does not jump up as a lion to fall down as a mouse. These reflections follow closely what Sextus himself says about the social relations of the sceptic. If we allow ourselves to depart from his narrative in secondary matters, a different picture may emerge. Thus, today, we would concede that absence of belief in truth may well combine with strong convictions.

As a fourth major category of criteria, Jahoda lists *autonomy*, the individual's degree of independence from social influences. Maslow speaks about people who maintain 'a relative serenity and happiness in the midst of circumstances that would drive other people to suicide'. David Riesman distinguishes between adjustment to society of the tradition-directed, inner-directed, and other-directed kinds and judges autonomy of the individual with reference to these factors. This is highly relevant for scepticism and justifies a brief digression.

It has often been noted that men of letters with sceptical inclinations tend to support the traditions of their society, and are, as a matter of course, never seduced by programmes of radical reform. They are conservative. It is the radical who accepts general propositions predicting the future.

David Hume, considered the most consistent philosophical sceptic since antiquity, was conservative as a matter of course. But what about his autonomy? Hume's autonomy in relation to the society he supported showed itself in many ways. An example of a rather touching kind is to be found in his relation to Rousseau. An individual belonging to quite a different society, a society of in part opposite character, Rousseau was, moreover, a person of diametrically opposite character and tastes. Hume nevertheless felt himself capable of sincere friendship with Rousseau, to the extent of inviting him to live in England with him. The story presents a convincing picture of a sceptic living at peace with his own society, but without self-surrender.

How would a sceptic behave under a tyrant, subjected to a terror régime? In our time this is a question that will inevitably be raised. Will he not be among the passive, at the best? Will he not be among those who are unable to fight for a principle, who let themselves be made instruments of criminal deeds?

In *Against the Ethicists*, a fundamental attack on the Wise Man of Greek philosophical traditions, Sextus answers dogmatists who think that a sceptic will either meekly surrender to a tyrant or stand up against him, but then on the basis of a conviction about what is good or evil, or desirable and undesirable, and thus inconsistently. A sceptic must either act dishonourably or be inconsistent. Sextus questions the dogmatic assumption that the capability of desiring some things and avoiding others presumes a *doctrine* of some kind, a belief in knowing this or that to be the case. Life can be lived without that. If the tyrant tries to compel a sceptic to do a forbidden act, he will refuse on the basis of laws and customs. Today we will perhaps add 'and according to conscience' (whether in agreement or in disagreement with the laws and customs of the time and place). Sextus adds that the sceptic will endure hardships more easily because of his lack of beliefs *about* suffering—beliefs that cause additional suffering.[1]

The inadequacy of an individual perception is clearly manifested in many neuroses, 'the neurotic is not only emotionally sick—he is cognitively *wrong*'—to quote Maslow again. As a fifth proposed

[1] See *Against the Ethicists*, trans. R. G. Bury (Loeb Classical Library, W. Heinemann, London 1936), pp. 160-7.

category of criteria, this point must be considered for a moment. The sceptic does not *deny* the distinction between correct and incorrect perception, it is just that he does not find *in practice* any indisputable criterion of correctness. In this he does not seem to feel very different from Marie Jahoda, who exclaims: 'Particularly when the object of perception is social in nature—but even when it is physical stimuli—who is to say what is "correct"?' Further, she intimates that correctness carries the implication that reality is static and limited and that there is only one way of looking at it.

In the face of this unexpected and remarkable support for the healthiness of a sceptical outlook, I find it justifiable to proceed to the last criterion, *environmental mastery*. There is one proposal here which directly affects the sceptic, that of making the capacity to *solve* problems a criterion. The sceptic admits that as a person he is incapable of finding the solution of any problem whatsoever in terms of true and false. He would fail dismally as a respondent to the innumerable true/false questionnaires of our cognitively atomistic and optimistic age. Jahoda comes to his aid here too, however, suggesting that it is rather the *process* of solving than the end product which discloses the healthy mind. Success in solving cannot count for such. The process or method itself does not imply any assertion with a truth-claim attached, and I think nothing can be said in general here against the sceptic.

Sextus himself was very probably a physician, one of the long line of Hellenic physicians systematically opposed to all philosophizing in medicine. The so-called empirical school tried to keep as close as possible to empirical methods, suspicious of any generalization or deduction and of any attempt to find causes. As a sceptic the medical problem-solver would also have to be critical of conceptualization of the relation between patient and doctor, favouring direct interaction at the non-conceptual level.

Our general conclusion from this confrontation of the sceptical philosopher with criteria of positive mental health must, I think, be very tentative, but at the same time positive. It is that there is no good *a priori* or general reason to suppose that a sceptic cannot stand up to current criteria of positive health.

The sceptic's failure may seem to come more easily from social rather than psychological sources: in a society which puts heavy stress on verbal conformity in the form of unconditional, explicit acceptance of ideological items in terms of true or false, the sceptic is likely to suffer maladjustment and consequent loss of peace of mind. Still, we have learned in our time how people under totalitarian pressure are capable of combining a high degree of external conformity with deep inner reservations. The sceptic may resort to a form of 'double-think', as do so many in all societies we know of.

3. ALLEGED SCEPTICISM OF ST. AUGUSTINE AND OTHERS

In his story of how sceptics develop, Sextus tells us how some gifted people fail to find decisive evidence either for or against any philosophical position. Contemporary psychologists will, I imagine, be justified in pronouncing that there must be a strong *propensity* towards finding counterarguments in order not to become convinced. There must be peculiar personality traits which explain the genesis of a sceptic. It cannot be a matter of pure intellect, or pure chance.

But what traits? If, drawing upon philosophy or the history of ideas, one could provide clear information on sceptical personalities of the past,[1] discussion on scepticism and mental health would be greatly simplified. But such information cannot be given.

Let me take an example of a type of literature containing reports of deep scepticism. It begins with St. Augustine (354–430), who says of himself that at about the age of thirty he had developed a complete scepticism. He doubted everything and gave up looking for any single truth (in the manner of the Academicians). He was profoundly unhappy, he lived in sin, and being torn between contrary impulses, had great difficulty in acting coherently. Unhappiness and scepticism thus went together.

All this he reports in his famous *Confessions*, after he had found peace in Christ, that is, after a religious conversion. Now, we know that people after a profound religious or political conversion tend to be very inaccurate in their descriptions of their own life before that happening. There is reason to believe that St. Augustine was no exception, and in particular that he was not as sceptical as he says he was.

If this is not the case, we would conclude that marked scepticism of the 'Academic' (not Pyrrhonian) kind is at least sometimes

---

[1] By 'sceptical personalities' I mean here 'personalities with a more or less pronounced sceptical bent of mind'. I am not thinking only of persons adhering to the radical scepticism of Sextus.

empirically connected *not* with peace of mind but with a state of deep frustration, indecisiveness, and with moral confusion.

Since Augustine a long series of Christian personalities have reported on the scepticism (that is, 'scepticism' in their own terminologies) that was theirs before their ultimate conversion. Some have even retained the point of view that they *are* sceptics. But it is clear that their concept of religious belief and of revelation is such that they must be said to claim at least to know the truth of every proposition of the Bible. They accept revelation as a source of knowledge of many kinds and confine their scepticism to propositions arrived at without revelation.

I have mentioned religious conversion as one current or movement in the history of ideas only as an example to illustrate the difficulties in assessing the personality background of a sceptical bent of mind. Even if that background were elucidated, it remains to assess the likelihood that a trait found associated with non-Pyrrhonian scepticism would also be associated with the 'suspension of judgment' variety. Conclusions on the psychological and social aspects of scepticism must therefore primarily be taken from the experience of contemporary psychologists and social scientists.

It seems quite likely that converts who have overcome their harrowing doubts tend to regard scepticism in the same light as do many psychotherapists and psychiatrists. For these latter 'scepticism' is often made to cover certain defence mechanisms of the unhealthy mind. The patient meets the environment, including the benevolent doctor, with constant irony, sarcasm, stubborn or blind doubt. He uses a sceptical phraseology to defend himself, to ward off any attempt to influence him in directions in which he does not want to be influenced. From his behaviour and utterances, however, it is clear that his sceptical phraseology is not based on a deep and genuine scepticism. The patient accepts many things as true and valid, for instance, as a submissive or loyal member of a gang. Or, he has a tendency to reject many things as false.

The psychiatric patient may even show symptoms of compulsive doubt, *Zweifelsucht*. In psychiatric literature there are examples of psychotic *Zweifelsucht* in which the patient fights between belief and doubt in certain metaphysical positions.[1] There is no develop-

---

[1] Karl Jaspers describes a case with obvious relevance for studies of states of *deep and general doubt* (*Allgemeine Psychopathologie* [4th edn., B. G. Teubner, Berlin, 1946], pp.

ment of confidence and trust with such patients, at least not as described by the psychiatrists. Their development, especially in this respect, differs widely from that of the Pyrrhonist.

The psychopathology of doubt, indecision, perplexity, disbelief, suspicion, mistrust is of interest to any student of sceptical tendencies, especially sceptical stages before religious conversions. But the pictures drawn by psychiatrists bear very little resemblance to those drawn by Sextus. The Pyrrhonist is certainly very different from the psychopathic nihilist and negativist, and also from the patients who are tortured by rapid wavering or oscillation between belief and disbelief.

4. MODERATE OR FRAGMENTARY SCEPTICISM OF THE UNPHILOSOPHICAL

In spite of the description of the sceptical way in the first part of this book, it is difficult to get a real feeling of what kind of person the sceptic is. We are invited to keep only certain rather limited characteristics in mind, the seven points of the genesis, but at the same time we want to supplement the account in such a way that a whole person emerges. I shall therefore devote the remainder of this chapter to clearing up some points regarding the sceptical bent of mind—and independently of whether the sceptic is a philosopher.

Dogmatic philosophers will, of course, confront the sceptic with specimens of the knowledge that is generally considered most certain. In order to be able to meet other philosophers on their own battleground, the philosophical sceptic must therefore furnish possible counterarguments against such sentences as 'I feel hot now' or 'I think, therefore I am', in so far as they are posed as assertions involving the claim that they express certain or probable knowledge.

But the unphilosophical sceptic, of at least one kind, will not bother with these sentences, taking it for granted that mostly they express something that is true, but trivial. Or else, as many non-philosophers do, he will deny the general applicability of the

---

112 ff.). It is plain from Karl Jaspers's classification of the sceptical frame of mind in his *Psychologie der Weltanschauungen* (4th edn., B. G. Teubner, Berlin, 1954), that his own psychopathological experience colours his perception of philosophical scepticism. Scepticism is classed as a form of nihilism and is clearly taken to be a form of deep and general doubt, incompatible with mental health.

term 'true' to the trivial or 'too obvious'. His scepticism is complete in its way if it comprises all knowledge *worth knowing*, all that he ever sincerely wished he knew. I think here of religious and moral doctrines and the unphilosophical sceptic's opinions on his own basic relations to his nearest family and friends. If he is rudely disappointed and frustrated because of opposing opinions on such things, his genesis as a sceptic can be the same as that of the philosophical sceptic described by Sextus. And if it is seen from a psychological and social point of view, the unphilosophical brand of scepticism will be complete and meaningful in spite of its fragmentary character from a strict cognitive point of view.

Suppose the complete but unphilosophical sceptic is led into philosophy and that he concedes that we have certain knowledge of a perceptual and of a purely logical kind. This does not require him to change his psychological and social status as a sceptic. If the concessions to the dogmatists are sufficiently remote from questions in which he is seriously and personally engaged, these concessions are without deeper effect. He is now moderately and fragmentarily sceptical as a professional philosopher, but still a complete sceptic in relation to all things worth knowing.

Whereas moderate, loose, or fragmentary scepticisms are scorned by the philosopher-epistemologists, they are central to *our* theme: the social and psychological aspects of scepticism. If we were to consider today only the radical, neatly, and professionally worked out brands of scepticism, we would feel rather as if we were discussing the intimate life of an extremely rare, possibly long extinct, species of bird.

But now, with this philosophically moderate and fragmentary yet psycho-socially total or near-total brand of scepticism in view, I shall proceed to some rather bold speculations.

5. ENCOURAGING A SCEPTICAL BENT OF MIND: CAN IT EVER BE RIGHT?

In cases of deep and painful doubt and oscillation between opposite views, the therapist should, it seems, represent the dogmatist rather than the sceptic. That is, he or she must help the patient towards a stable view, a valid positive conclusion, whether or not valid in the eyes of the therapist. This may also apply to young people drifting along the stream, and with little feeling of identity, or of anything that is truly expressive of themselves.

They may look like potential (Pyrrhonian) sceptics, but they are not likely to become so. They have not gone through the pre-sceptical stage of asking 'What is truth?' with strength and endurance. And therefore the sceptic's peace of mind cannot be theirs.

Admitting, however, that in many cases a tendency towards scepticism should *not* be encouraged, what are the cases in which it should or at least might?

Let us consider a young man called Max. He is brought up in a highly intellectual atmosphere with stress on articulated opinions justifying attitudes and actions. It is never enough for him to say 'That's the way I feel now', 'I cannot help valuing this higher than that', 'I just like it', 'This, not that, is my duty', and so on; there must be reasons and claims of objective truth and validity. For various reasons Max has early developed a keen critical sense, *contra*-argument coming to him more naturally than *pro*-argument. And this criticalness, owing to a not too greatly developed sense of superiority, comes as easily to him in respect of his *own* tentative positions as in respect of those of others.

Without being intellectually inferior, Max is constantly in trouble because he cannot form enduring verbalized convictions and because his father and others who try to press him into certain beliefs are largely immune to counterarguments relating to their own positions. When Max has to make decisions in school, as a student, as a friend, and in relation to the other sex, he insists on making positions conscious, and on justifying them intellectually. He demands that his own actions should always be based on considerations of truth, correctness, and worthwhile consequences.

Any effort to change the old trait Max has of coming to see two sides of a thing, and his tendency towards detached objectivity and valid reasoning, is liable to fail just because this feature is so deeply engrained. And, of course, few therapists would have the audacity to interfere with it, since from many points of view such a trait is an asset. However, the case is one in which help towards a more complete scepticism is warranted. What Max lacks may be said to be the courage to oppose those who make him feel that the intellectual articulation and justification of impulses is necessary, and who have implanted in him a distrust of action or attitude-formation without an accompaniment of intellectual justification in terms of truth and general validity. The sceptical outlook involves a mistrust in such justifications and a capacity to see their hollowness from the point of view of intellectual detachment and honesty. Instead of feeling that this ability to see counterarguments is shameful and expressive of inferiority, Max will be encouraged to exercise his ability and to stick to his resulting intellectual indecision and suspension of judgment.

It will perhaps be objected that Max's cure is basically one not of being led to accept and develop further his sceptical bent of mind but of being led to trust his own impulses.

However, the term 'scepticism' has been introduced in this text as it was by Sextus, that is, in terms of the genesis of a kind of personality. Essential in Sextus's narrative is his 'impression' that indecision, or rather suspension of judgment, as to truth and falsity does not result in inactivity. Natural impulses lead to action. Upbringing, social institutions, teachers in the arts provide a sufficient basis for adjustment, both for the passive component, the accommodation, and the active, the assimilation, in the terminology of Piaget. Thus trust in one's own impulses is an integral part of the scepticism expressed by Sextus Empiricus.

An essential kind of question for Max is 'How did I come to think that in order to decide whether to go to college or not I would have to solve the question whether an interesting or lucrative job is the best for me? Or whether there is a duty for intelligent men today to go to college in order that in 1980 the United States may have more able engineers than the Soviet Union and China put together?' Max would have to train himself to have a sharp awareness of his own inclinations, develop his sensitivity, get his impulses co-ordinated, and use his intellectual acumen to reveal for himself the unwarranted jumps from particular, concrete personal questions to more general and abstract ones, and to distinguish innocent verbalizations ('What beautiful places some college campuses are!') from more formidable articulations in terms of truth and validity.

Let us, once more, look for personality traits correlated with a profoundly sceptical bent of mind. Let us consider a middle-aged intellectually gifted person called Adam. Adam has long had a need for a unified outlook on life of the kind which Gordon Allport takes to be a sign of health. And as far as we, his psychologist friends, are able to judge, he *had* a highly unified all-pervading outlook when he was twenty-five years old. When he had that outlook he seemed to thrive. Then he became married to a headstrong girl, Mary, with a different outlook. Unhappily there developed much friction and Adam was gradually led to *carefully articulate his own outlook*, articulation functioning mainly as a defence mechanism.

Articulation presupposes a certain degree of alienation from oneself, a dangerous kind of objectivity. Adam was led to look at himself from the outside and to make clear other possibilities than his own outlook. There now developed a profound indecision and general doubt, and Adam proceeded to undergo an analysis of a somewhat orthodox Freudian kind. It was soon clear that the need of a unified outlook developed out of earlier conflicts, when he was torn between father and mother. His outlook represented a victory of the father image, but there must be something left over, something incompletely integrated in his personality. This explains why his infatuation for Mary had the serious consequence of marriage, in spite of the incongruence between the two in the matter of outlook.

The analysis was highly successful. To put it in terms of symbols, the main result was that he saw that he no longer needed to choose between mother and father. On the contrary, he felt the arbitrariness of any choice of that kind. Transferred to the field of conscious behaviour, it meant a rejection of unified outlooks, a natural disinclination to let himself fasten on to any decision in terms of outlooks on life or anything else. Confronted with believers in the truth of any religion, philosophy, or political ideology, counterarguments developed, in a natural way, in his mind. Having William James as a distant relative, he often justified his renunciation of knowledge in terms of pragmatism, but he did not really believe in pragmatism. He used pragmatic patterns of argumentation because they were the most convenient way of cutting off reflections leading nowhere.

Whatever the genesis of a definite general outlook, it cannot be shed like a coat. It is therefore not surprising to hear from the psychologist friends of Adam that his social and physical perceptions still have a peculiar tone or colour consistent with his former highly integrated outlook. The difference is that he will not stand up and defend his impressions and reactions as any more valid or true than any other. He trusts his impulses but his intellectualizations have disintegrated, leaving only the minimum necessary for adjustment to his social environment.

Today I surmise that there are many psychotherapists who are not far from scepticism in their basic attitudes, however full of certainty they may sometimes be in their speech. This makes it easier to help unburden over-intellectualized minds of unnecessary, unending reflections about truth and falsity, validity and invalidity. I should think therefore that scepticism of the radical kind we are discussing should not be wholly without practical importance for psychotherapy, hence that here at least is one context in which it may be considered practically desirable. The relevance in wider contexts of a conclusion about the practical value of scepticism in this one field must be left to those who would consider in more detail the connection between mental health and community, and the importance of a sceptical attitude among those who would seek to influence the development of society. One might reasonably predict important social implications of widespread scepticism, even of the fragmentary, unphilosophical kind. It should effectively undermine closed societies with their demands for explicit adherence to certain doctrines and the systematic rejection of counterargument. And in more or less open societies scepticism should help both in the reshuffling of political priorities and in the elimination of rigid ideological reasoning that lacks any basis in spontaneous thought and feeling.

IV

CONCEPTUAL COMPLEMENTARITY OF EVIDENCE AND TRUTH REQUIREMENTS

1. INTRODUCTION

KNOWLEDGE implies truth: What is known cannot be false. This is a matter of definition. There are other requirements too. In the usual case knowledge that so-and-so is not attributable to someone who truly believes something unless that person has reason for his belief. But even this is not quite enough, since a true belief based on reasons might still be rejected as knowledge if the reasons were not considered adequate. That is, for a true belief to be knowledge the reasons or grounds for holding it must satisfy certain standards. Some people put this by saying that knowledge is a title that beliefs must earn, and that they earn it not simply by being true but by being well grounded.

In taking up these points we shall depart from the course generally taken in discussions on scepticism. Usually the epistemologist concerned with scepticism is occupied with general questions of the form 'Do our beliefs ever earn the title of knowledge?' Ayer, for example, in *The Problem of Knowledge*, presents the sceptic as one who alleges that our reasons for believing that so-and-so can never be good enough for the belief in question to count as knowledge, the argument being that a knowledge claim involves an 'illegitimate inference' from one level of facts, which form the premises of our knowledge claim, to another level of facts which forms the conclusion.[1] The problem, as Ayer sees it, is that of establishing our right to make what appears to be a special sort of advance beyond our data.[2] In the case of our belief in the existence of the external world, for example, the sceptic is represented as maintaining 'that we have no access to physical objects otherwise than through the contents of our sense-ex-

[1] A. J. Ayer, *The Problem of Knowledge*, p. 76. [2] *Ibid.*, p. 78.

periences, which themselves are not physical' and that since the relationship between premises and conclusion is neither an inductive nor a deductive one the inference cannot be justified. If our beliefs about the existence of physical objects can never be justified the existence of physical objects can never be known.

Here, however, we will consider not the transition from a true belief to a justified true belief but the transition from a belief that is justified to a belief that is both justified and true. That is, we shall consider the interrelationship of the truth and evidence requirements of knowledge, a change of focus that brings to light a 'problem of knowledge' rather different from that normally discussed, a problem of adequately conceptualizing expressions of the form 'I know that p' in terms of truth and evidence. The import of the following discussion will be that there are difficulties in giving any consistent analysis of knowledge expressions when these are used purportedly to convey information that there is evidence for the truth of some assertion, and that that assertion is true. These difficulties suggest that certain limits are imposed on the usefulness of knowledge expressions, a conclusion which would provide philosophical support for the radical sceptic's disinclination to affirm the truth of anything.

However, as in all arguments, the limits of our conclusions are as important as the conclusions themselves, and it will be necessary to note the restrictions that are imposed on them by the nature of the problem of knowledge as we conceive it. In particular we shall have to guard against inferring from the fact that there are difficulties in giving a satisfactory account of knowledge expressions in terms of truth and evidence (or ground), to the conclusion that these difficulties are in some sense 'inherent in the very notion of knowledge'. As we shall see, there is no obvious connection between these difficulties and questions about whether knowledge is possible or not, that is, with the problem of knowledge as ordinarily conceived. On the other hand, they do have a bearing on the acceptability or possibility of radical scepticism, and the following discussion constitutes an attempted justification of radical scepticism. (As such, of course, it is not a justification that the radical sceptic could consistently accept; but if he was favourably impressed by the arguments he might well employ them as counterarguments against those who dogmatically assert his own intellectual unresponsibility.)

The nature of the 'problem of knowledge' as discussed here

can be expressed in terms of the awkwardness of applying knowledge expressions when one takes into consideration the combined truth and evidence requirements of such expressions. This awkwardness can be expressed in terms of a secondary thesis which asserts the impossibility of identifying an event which constitutes the transition from reaching towards knowledge to grasping it. In fact, the metaphor of reaching, as also of arriving at, cannot be applied to any use of knowledge expressions which explicitly differentiates the truth requirement from the evidence requirement. To put it summarily, we might say that knowledge cannot be reached in such a sense, by any increase of evidence.

2. RESTRICTIONS AND QUALIFICATIONS

Some restrictions and qualifications have to be made to the above theses. First, I provide no arguments to show that those concepts of knowledge according to which knowledge definitely implies or definitely does not imply truth and evidence are the *only ones* possible. For example, I shall not attempt in this inquiry to refute certain versions of pragmatism and subjectivism. There is, however, general agreement that it is the concepts of knowledge which imply truth and evidence that are the important ones in philosophical discourse. This seems to have been acknowledged ever since Plato.[1] Apparently Plato and Aristotle did not doubt that such knowledge could be and had been reached. Aristotle indeed is very specific in contending that knowledge of this kind is derived through evidence. Thus, one of his theses might be formulated as follows: In at least one sense of 'knowledge' and 'reaching', knowledge implying truth and evidence is something which we *can* reach through an increase in evidence.

Secondly, although our secondary thesis about 'reaching' does

[1] Apparently Plato could only explain how such knowledge is generated by recourse to theories or myths about remembering: knowledge is not reached, but found introspectively in a way in which reaching for it is not called for.

Aristotle in no way weakens the 'Platonic' requirement that knowledge should comprise an absolute relationship to truth: quite the contrary, he explicitly and repeatedly affirms that what is known is true and that such knowledge (*epistémé*) is incorrigible. We only know things about which we *cannot* be mistaken. If truth is claimed, a kind of incorrigibility claim must follow (cf. *Eth. Nic.* 1139b 15–36). To say 'I know it but *it* may be false' is strange, at best. I may admit that as a human being I am always fallible, but if I say 'I know that *p*', I must claim that *p*'s truth is incorrigible, or that I cannot even make sense of attributing corrigibility or incorrigibility to *truth*. A belief, a working hypothesis, is corrigible, but if *p* is accepted only as a good working hypothesis, I would not say 'I know that *p*'.

apply also to 'arriving at', it is not intended to cover a thesis about 'having'. It is at least not clear that the inability to conceptualize arrival at knowledge entails the impossibility of having knowledge. Therefore the possibility that we do in fact know a great deal certainly cannot be excluded. All that is denied is that we can give any consistent account of our arrival at whatever knowledge we may have, and may have obtained.

Further, in many cases the question of evidence and the description of steps of accumulation of evidence seem out of place. With respect to certain kinds of everyday utterances, we scarcely talk about evidence, collecting more evidence, and the like, at all. For instance, I do not speak about my evidence for believing that this is my finger, or that it is not raining on this table. In the case of it being irrelevant to ask about evidence, the question of how to arrive at knowledge by an increase in evidence does not arise. In what follows I intend to talk about utterances in relation to which it *is* relevant to ask such questions as 'What about the evidence?', 'How do you know?', 'What makes you so sure?', 'How did you find out?', and so on. Thus, if I say I am in pain, the situation is mostly of a kind that makes the quest for evidence or certainty irrelevant or at least very queer. It will be noticed that this limits our discussions appreciably compared to that of Sextus and our own treatment of Sextus in Chap. I. Sextus discusses at length such sentences as 'I feel hot now' and other utterances which in everyday life are not supposed ever to elicit a 'What is your evidence (for such a conclusion)?' The question 'What *kinds* of statement or what kinds of circumstances are such that the question of evidence is irrelevant or inappropriate?' is, of course, a formidable one, and cannot be taken up here. Some philosophers, J. L. Austin among them, favour broad delimitations of the field of inappropriateness (see, e.g., *Sense and Sensibilia* [Clarendon Press, Oxford], pp. 115 ff.).

3. SHIFT FROM PLAIN ANNOUNCEMENT OF KNOWLEDGE TO JUSTIFYING CLAIM TO SAY ONE KNOWS

To claim that knowledge cannot be reached may seem counter-intuitive. Perhaps it will be protested that there are cases in which it seems utterly clear that knowledge *is* reached, and by an increase in evidence. Until recently, for example, there was only relatively indirect evidence in support of the existence of high mountains on the other side of the moon. But then photographs became available. Surely, then, we can say that it is true that there are mountains, and that we know it, and that truth and knowledge were reached some years ago through a definite increase in evidence? If there is a problem here it seems only to be that of the paradox of the heap, that is, of determining at what step of the accumulation the evidence became sufficient to establish truth, with which photograph and at what stage in its production somebody grasped the truth and thus acquired the knowledge that 'there are high mountains on the other side of the moon'. But if one looks a little closer into the matter, the problem confronting the epistemologist appears more involved.

The way in which people use expressions of the form 'N.N. knows that p' suggests a model in terms of which certain situations serve as ideal examples. The model of knowing that p is that, let us say, of being in the special kind of cognitive position or vantage point *vis-à-vis* the facts that we assume to obtain in the case of seeing things. When I say I know that something is the case, it is because I believe I am aware of the facts in some way analogous to direct perception of them; I and the facts are in the same sort of excellent cognitive relation. Just as I have things or events in view, so I have facts in my grasp. And just as I came to see things or events with my eyes, so I came to grasp the facts with my mind.

Thus prior to the photographs of the back of the moon the facts were not grasped, but now that they are available the fact that there are mountains there is a piece of knowledge in the hands of at least certain scientists and also perhaps of those who have seen or been told about the pictures.

The plausibility of this way of talking rests on the acceptance of certain situations as instances of the paradigm cognitive relationship. It is assumed that in certain situations we have not merely better evidence, but that the evidence we have is so good as to be tantamount to, or in some sense to guarantee, truth.

But it seems that to treat a situation as one in which truth recognizably accompanies the evidence involves an evasion or a denial of a basic fact: and that is that truth and evidence are *complementary* requirements of knowledge. Now, to describe these two requirements as complementary is simply to say that in order for 'p is known' to be true there must be acceptable evidence for p, and p must be true. There is, it seems, nothing inconsistent in the assumption that the two requirements are on any occasion separately satisfied; to assert that p may be known is meaningful and consistent. But there is no way in which this can be more than an assumption. It is not possible, so far as I can see, to give an account of some situation in which that situation can be described as furnishing either two sets of denotata answering to the truth and evidence requirements or one set of denotata which truth and evidence share. There is in fact no identifiable situation answering to the paradigm cognitive relationship which knowledge claims assume and the assumption of which lies at the basis of the utility of knowledge expressions.

These considerations can be seen to emerge when pressure is applied to everyday uses of 'I know' and similar expressions. Ordinary run-of-the-mill claims to know that something or other is the case are generally unproblematic. There are fairly clearly defined rules for making such claims, and for accepting or rejecting them. That is, expressions like 'I know' function satisfactorily for communication. But it seems that the utility of such expressions depends on the assumption or convention that evidence of a certain kind does constitute or guarantee truth, and hence knowledge. However, when pressure, even if only in the form of attention, comes to bear on this assumption, the complementarity of truth and evidence is exposed and the utility of the expressions rapidly diminishes.

When, for whatever reason, people go into the details of the evidence, considering one piece at a time, I think most of them, whether they are philosophically sophisticated or not, tend (1) to stop using the distinctions between known and not-known and between true and untrue, or (2) to shift towards the question of being *justified in asserting or saying* 'Now it is true' or 'Now it is known'. That is, there is a tendency to estimate what might be, from a social point of view, sufficient to *claim* this or that. 'Nobody' will *blame* anybody for *saying* 'It is true that there are mountains on the other side of the moon, and at least some photographers are directly aware of the fact'.

If, experimentally, we press people towards retaining the above distinctions, the results indicate a shift towards *increasing indefinitely* the requirements for grasping knowledge and for guarantees of truth. 'Of course one cannot be absolutely sure', 'Naturally, there is always a chance of being mistaken', and so on. Such increases in the requirements do not necessarily affect the consistency or constancy of the meaning of 'truth' and of 'knowledge' in everyday talk. The shifts are just part of the way the terms are used, and consist in certain terms being dropped and others used in their place. A sort of verbal evasion takes place: repeated posings of the question 'Do you *know*?' after a while no longer elicit answers in terms of knowledge but in terms of evidence, 'untranslatable' into answers in terms of reaching knowledge.

The transition from knowledge expressions to evidence expressions, the substantial increases or decreases of requirements, and concessions such as 'Of course, one cannot be absolutely sure' which do *not* imply retraction of a previous 'I know it', all these complicated mechanisms affecting daily use are relevant to attempts to delimit a meaning or connotation, or a set of meanings and connotations of 'knowing'. Being conceptually indeterminate, so to speak, these mechanisms are not of a kind easily taken care of in ordinary definitions and explicit conceptual determinations (*Begriffsbestimmungen*) and are not easily adapted to formulation in terms of sets of constant requirements, criteria, or necessary conditions.

The same kind of shifts can be studied in other cases: something is said to be known *now* but not to have been known at a previous date, and the difference is readily said to be due to an increase of evidence. But if, contrary to custom, detailed information is elicited concerning the way the difference was established, concerning the dates and the documentation, and so on, there is a shift in the actual theme of the discussion, from *being* true and known to *saying* that something is true and known. Or, from knowing to having evidence of this or that kind.

The distinction between asking 'Is *p* true?' and 'Is it justifiable to say (assert) *p*?' is a well established one both in everyday life and in scientific contexts. 'You may say you are occupied (or not feeling well, unable to answer, etc.)', that is, you may say these things even if you know they are untrue. 'It is perfectly justifiable to say you have found the solution', to say that you *believe* you have found it will give listeners a wrong impression; they will underestimate the evidence you have, or assume you have none.

However, claiming that a difference is well established in everyday life and in scientific contexts does not necessarily imply that the definiteness of intention in communication is always sufficient to allow for the distinction to be intended. In fact, the distinction between 'Is p true?' and 'Is it justifiable to assert p?' is often slurred over, and in recent philosophical discussions this practice has received some encouragement, as we shall see. However, although there are well-established precedents both for making the distinction and for ignoring it, in what follows we must rely on the distinction being made with great emphasis.

The conclusion drawn from empirical studies of cases in which people actually use the terms 'true', 'known', and 'evidence' is, in short, *not* that they tend explicitly to *give up* or retract their claim to know, or that they soften the truth requirement, but that they continue the discussion as if the claim had not been made. The truth and knowledge claims are left alone: the speakers leave one subject of discussion for another. Or so, at least, it appears from the point of view of the epistemologist. But of course a shift of ground is always relative to someone's, usually theoretically determined, partitioning of the ground, and it is no doubt possible to redraw the boundaries in such a way that we should say there was no shift of ground.

Let us none the less conclude that, at least from the point of view of an epistemologist who will not allow that situations may arise in which the known/not-known distinction is inapplicable or can be misplaced, there is indeed a shift of ground, a *metabasis eis allo genos*.

4. REQUIREMENTS OF 'KNOWING' INVOLVING THREE QUESTIONS—CORRESPONDING QUESTIONNAIRES

There is, in recent philosophical discussions, a flourishing branch of the family of definitions, or sets of definitions, of knowledge, namely those requiring three things: that one be sure, that one have adequate grounds for being sure, and that what is claimed to be known be true.[1]

---

[1] Other representative subfamilies of such truth-requiring concepts of knowledge can be introduced by variation of interpretation of the sign '$=$' in a formula '$A = B$' where 'A' is 'He knows that p' and 'B' is 'He is sure that p, he has adequate grounds for being sure, and p is true'. In this way the following kinds of sentences (among others) are constructed:
  (1) 'A means the same as B.'
  (2) 'The criterion of A is B.'
  (3) 'The necessary and sufficient condition of A is B.'
As an example of an individual member of the family we may take the following: 'He knows that it rains' means the same as 'He is sure that p, he has adequate grounds

I shall try in what follows to break through the barriers between epistemological discussion and empirical observation by asking: What would happen if we tried *to use* the three requirements in actual situations, if we asked whether a particular given statement fulfilled them?

Now any actual use of three such complicated items makes it necessary to apply them one at a time. But then this has a very serious consequence: instead of a question that is timeless and abstract, we get one in which the order in which two separate items are applied matters. There will now be *three* questions of the kind 'Does this statement fulfil requirement *x*?'

The three items may be interpreted as three necessary conditions. Together they have been considered to make up a complete set of necessary and sufficient conditions. And every time anybody rightly concludes that he or somebody else knows something it is presumed that *the three questions have been given adequate answers*, one for each necessary condition.

Let us call a standard set of questions asked in a definite, repeatable kind of situation a 'questionnaire'. The requirements, if used explicitly, will then delimit a family of questionnaires. It seems that such a questionnaire cannot easily be avoided if, contrary to custom, the requirements are to be used or put forward explicitly in concrete cases, one after the other. Persons who want to act responsibly and to make sure that they themselves or others *know* that such-and-such is the case will have to remind themselves of the three questions, listing them in one of the six possible orders.

---

for being sure, and *p* is true'. The expression 'means the same as' can be made more precise in various directions, for instance, by introducing references to person and situation: '*A* means for P_1 in S_1 the same as *B* for P_2 in S_2'; or by introducing criteria of synonymity of various degrees of strength. In what follows it is largely (but certainly not totally) irrelevant how the schema '*A* = *B*' is interpreted. At least three possible functions should be distinguished: (1) use of the requirements for decisions concerning the *social or ethical justification* for calling, or of having called, a proposition knowledge. 'You said you knew the gun was unloaded; were you entitled to do so, did you have adequate grounds?'; (2) use of the requirements as a *criterion* or *reminder* when deciding whether *p* is known or not; (3) use in *defining* what is meant by '*p* is known'. The set of three requirements may function more or less well in these ways. But these functions must be carefully distinguished. It is dangerously misleading if, for example, one applies the requirements in ways (2) and (3) to our own momentary decisions.

5. THE 'THIRD-PERSON' AND 'FIRST-PERSON' QUESTIONNAIRES

If I am asked 'Does N.N. *know* that Leif Ericsson discovered America?', I may decide to use the following kind of questionnaire:[1]

(1) Question 1: Is he sure that p?
Question 2: Does he have adequate grounds for being sure?
Question 3: Is p true?

In Questionnaire (1) the third question is clearly different from the conjunction of Questions 1 and 2, provided 'adequate' is defined in terms of certain (social) standards.

But now we come to the problem children of our distinguished family, the criteria that *I* know that p:

(2) I know that p—I am sure that p, I have adequate grounds for being sure that p, and p is true.

On questioning myself, or being questioned by others, as to whether I know p to be the case, what am I to do when confronted by the third requirement? What is the relation between the first two and the third for me who am on the point of deciding whether I do or do not know that p is the case?

Is it really a new question? And if so, what can I provide in answer to it except repetitions of what I have already said?

For the sake of an easy survey, both the third-person questionnaire, where I answer questions about another person, and the first-person questionnaire, where I answer questions about myself, may be formulated thus:

(3) Question 1: Is he sure that p?	Am I sure that p?
Question 2: Does he have adequate grounds for being sure that p?	Do I have adequate grounds for being sure that p?
Question 3: Is p true?	Is p true?

When deciding whether *he* knows, I answer the question 'Is p true?' on the authority of my own beliefs and grounds—a basis not referred to previously in the questionnaire. The 'third-person

---

[1] In many cases the question is closely related to such questions as 'Is N.N. aware of the fact that . . .' or 'Does N.N. know it or is he ignorant of it?' The questionnaire is not intended to take care of this usage.

questionnaire' is, so to speak, that of a bystander, an observer, or maybe an editor of an encyclopedia of knowledge, like the one compiled by Otto Neurath (whose views about knowledge were described by Bertrand Russell as characteristic of an editor, not a contributor).

On the other hand, when faced with the third question 'Is *p* true?' of the first-person questionnaire, I shall *once more* ask myself 'Do I have adequate grounds?', or search frantically for something more than evidence, say a guarantee of truth, a direct, transcendental insight into the nature of things. I must look for something that allows me to eliminate the *process* of knowing, of mediation. For I am no longer being asked about grounds; the positive answer to the question of adequacy of grounds remains unchallenged but seems not to be taken as sufficient.

If I have already answered 'Yes' to the question about adequate grounds, the question 'Is *p* true?' will then tend to be interpreted according to a strong or a weak interpretation of 'adequate grounds', either as an awkward repetition of the question concerning adequate grounds or as an undecidable question, such as 'Irrespective of my adequate grounds and my personal conviction, *is* there life on other planets?'

All through this discussion I have presumed that we are dealing with questions in relation to which the quest for evidence is relevant. In such cases I know of no other basis except evidence for establishing truth and (true) knowledge. But, then, the third question, the truth requirement, cannot be taken as an independent requirement when an individual judges his own knowledge claims. And in that case the third question is a misleading one.

This criticism of the set of three requirements for knowledge does not automatically apply to our consideration of the statements of *other* people. There we are bystanders, judges, sociologists, editors.

But maybe a simple change in the order of the stated requirements may save the three-requirement conceptions. Perhaps we should ask for truth first and evidence afterwards. R. M. Chisholm, in *Perceiving*,[1] treats the truth requirement, just as we have done so far, as the third requirement. But A. J. Ayer, in *The Problem of Knowledge*, puts the truth requirement first. He writes:

[1] *Perceiving, A Philosophical Study* (Cornell University Press, Ithaca, 1957).

'I conclude then that the necessary and sufficient conditions for knowing that something is the case are first that what one is said to know be true, secondly that one be sure of it, and thirdly that one should have the right to be sure.'[1]

Reformulated, this piece of text may well be taken as a member of the family of definitions under consideration, because Ayer makes the right to be sure depend upon the satisfaction of certain standards of evidence.[2]

A first-person questionnaire adapted to Ayer's point of view would run as follows:

(4) Question 1: Is what I say I know true?
    Question 2: Am I sure of what I say I know?
    Question 3: Do I have the right to be sure of what I say I know?

For the purpose of comparison with other questionnaires let us reformulate these questions as follows:

(5) Question 1: Is p true?
    Question 2: Am I sure that p?
    Question 3: Do I have the right to be sure that p?

As in the case of the expression 'adequate evidence', the expression 'right to be sure' admits of a strong and a weak interpretation, according to whether or not one only has the right to be sure that p, if p is true. In the former case truth is, in other words, taken to be a necessary condition for having the right to be sure, while in the latter case it is not. The two interpretations may be formulated thus:

T_0: adequate grounds
T_1: grounds which according to prevailing standards are sufficient to justify my being sure
T_2: grounds which are so good that if they are realized, then p is true

[1] Ayer, *The Problem of Knowledge*, p. 35.
[2] Efforts to make this formulation of Ayer's more precise soon evoke the question: Does Ayer intend by 'is the case' (in the phrase 'knowing that something is the case') something different from 'be true' (in 'to know to be true')? If not, the first part of his formulation can be reformulated thus: 'Thus necessary and sufficient conditions for knowing that something is the case are first that it *is* the case . . .'. The non-epistemological, purely ontological weight of 'to be the case' makes the expression better suited to bringing out the difference between the first and the third requirement. The expression 'to be true' has too many uses with epistemological shades. It very often resembles 'to be (to have been) verified'.

In the following I shall be assuming T_1 rather than T_2, that is, I adhere to the 'social standard' interpretation. A positive answer to Question 3, using T_2, amounts to a declaration that one acts as a responsible member of society. One can justify having answered positively, even if subsequent events should make it natural to conclude that p is false. This interpretation, in other words, provides for the eventuality that one was mistaken. If one was indeed mistaken, one nevertheless had the right to be sure.

The strong interpretation indeed is not the usual one among epistemologists. Thus, according to Ayer,[1] one earns the right independently of the question of what will actually happen later. Later one may earn the right to retract the original claim. The right to be sure that p and the right to be sure that not-p are earned at definite dates by definite people. Thus, at the same time as person A earns the right to be sure that p, B may earn the right to be sure that not-p. Hence, although the strong interpretation of 'adequate grounds' and 'right to be sure' makes the third question a repetition of the first, the weaker interpretation allows that one may have the right to be sure irrespective of the question of truth. That is, I may, for instance, have information which nobody can reasonably expect me to doubt, but which in a particular situation is misleading. Thus, I will not reject the remote possibility that I am now in Africa, but I shall insist that I have the right to be sure I am in Europe. My evidence fulfils, I firmly believe, any reasonable standard of evidence, and I shall turn with indignation towards anybody who questions that I have at least *the right to say* I know I am in Europe. I may concede remote possibilities of p being false and at the same time insist on having the right to say I know that p.

After this digression on the expressions 'right to be sure' and 'right to say I know', let us inspect our new formulation, (5); let us call it the modified Ayer-questionnaire.

As an oral questionnaire, it is likely to be more successful than the previous first-person questionnaires, because the subject asks himself directly about p *before* he asks about his personal relations to p. Ontology precedes epistemology.

Empirical investigations have shown, however, that people, when asked about their relations to p, that is, whether they are sure and what evidence they have, tend to give up the simple straightforward expressions 'It is true' and 'I know' in favour of

[1] Ayer, *The Problem of Knowledge*, p. 43.

such expressions as 'I am convinced it is true', 'I am perfectly sure it is true', or the even more subjective 'I am convinced' and 'I am perfectly sure'. Both logically and psychologically, this shift of ground is significant. Expressions which refer to our own relations to the proposition are used when our attention is focused on that relation. One may conclude, maybe on the next day, 'I was convinced it was true, but actually it was false', 'I was perfectly sure of it, but it was not so', or 'I was sure I knew, but I did not'. On the other hand, under these conditions one will not conclude 'It was true, but actually it was false', or 'I knew it, but it was false'. The difference is made even clearer if I say next day: 'I said yesterday that I was *convinced p* was true. I *was* convinced that it was true what I said. But, unfortunately, it turns out that *p* is false.'[1]

If, now, evidence increases, and even with the force of an avalanche, (perfectly normal) people tend to continue to use the evidence-centred expressions. They do not revert to the simple '*p* is true'. More than that, explications of truth in terms of maximal evidence seem to be self-defeating, because nobody seems to have described a kind of actual evidence possessed or enjoyed by some actual person such that the mere having or enjoying of it automatically establishes truth. Changing the order of the questions consequently does not solve our problem of how to find a natural first-person questionnaire that combines the impersonal truth requirement and the personal conviction and evidence requirement.

By empirical methods of research the shift from truth terminology to evidence terminology may be studied in detail. We shall see that it can be explained in terms of the conceptual framework of empirical semantics. However, before we attempt that we should perhaps accommodate those philosophers who are still reluctant to hand over to science what they can possibly discuss in their own terms, and try to put the facts into frameworks that are more familiar to them.

Of these the game framework is one of the most absorbing at the present time. One may conceive of a mother-game (or point-of-departure game), the simply-telling-what-is-the-case game which, when certain constellations are reached, can start off two

[1] It is interesting to note that positive answers to Questions 1 and 3 may, in a very natural way, be introduced by the phrase 'I am perfectly convinced that . . .', but not so the synthesis 'Do you *know* that *p*?'

mutually exclusive subgames, the truth-game and the evidence-game. One must make a choice at the appropriate point, and then there is no way back. If one chooses the truth-game one must stick to its own bleak and depersonalized terminology, using expressions without even an implicit reference to the problems and practices of justification, possibly just repeating the truth-claim. If one chooses the evidence-game one must describe, assess, and weigh evidence, using the complicated, rich vocabulary of the trades and sciences.

In choosing and playing the evidence-game one also starts off on a new round of the mother-game: weighing the evidence, you say that such-and-such *are* the sources of error, that some piece of evidence is better than another piece, and so on. If your partner introduces a knowledge-game ('How do you *know*?') in relation to your statements about the evidence, the crucial choice situation may turn up once again, and you will have to choose once more between the truth- and the evidence-game. But the new, subsidiary play does not ruin the principal one; you may just go ahead, continuing the moves appropriate for the situation.

So much for the applications of game concepts to the problem. But there is another popular framework among philosophers: the transition from truth to evidence or vice versa can also be conceived in terms of rationally reconstructed levels.

When my attention is absorbed by the process of amassing evidence, the use of the expression 'It is true' refers to second-order statements. Thus, I may say 'The evidence, it is true, has not increased to such an extent that it is simply crushing'. Or we may say 'I am now perfectly convinced. That is true'. Or we say 'Nobody can blame you, you were sure that the gun was unloaded. That is true. But you blundered when saying you *knew* it was unloaded'.

If, being already at the second level, I start to reflect, the terms not referring to evidence and conviction disappear. If I have said 'I am perfectly convinced, that is true', and I am questioned about the honesty of my conviction, I shall speak of my *evidence* of the sincerity of my conviction and this makes it difficult to revert to simply saying 'It is true that I am convinced'.

The simple phrasing 'It *is* true' may disappear only to reappear at the third level, and so forth.

Thus the shift from truth terminology to evidence terminology induced by applying the corresponding requirements separately

89

can be neatly conceptualized; that is to say, it is possible, in these terms, and no doubt in others, to provide a rational explanation of the change of ground. But what such conceptualizations so neatly express is precisely the disparity of the two requirements in their concrete application: the requirements, in short, are not *used* in such a way as to complement one another. One might say that the mistake such conceptualizations clearly point to is that of inferring from the correctness of an analysis of 'I know that p' in terms of two distinct requirements of truth and evidence, to the conclusion that we explicitly require of particular knowledge claims that they presuppose separate answers to questions about truth and evidence.

Now this is of relevance for the analyses provided by Ayer and others who accept the three-requirement concept of knowledge. As a piece of concept-mapping, or rational reconstruction, such analyses may be helpful, in so far as they abstract the logical implications of common usage. And yet, however faithfully these analyses represent the conceptual implications of 'I know that p', it is important to see that the details of the analyses do not necessarily reproduce conceptual distinctions actually made in common usage. This can be seen by applying such analyses to concrete cases.

Suppose someone, A, asserts that he knows that p. If 'I have adequate grounds for belief in p' and 'p is true' are said to express two conditions for such an assertion, the mere listing of them together by another person, B, in the presence of A, changes the whole atmosphere for A. The requirement expressed by 'p is true' is such that it cannot be added to 'I have adequate grounds for belief in p' without a change of attitude; when saying 'p is true' attention is fixed on that which is asserted by 'p'. The combination of the two conditions requires of A that he maintains a combined externalizing and non-externalizing attitude, or that he oscillates rapidly between the two.

How is A to interpret B's interference? In all likelihood A will interpret the second condition, the truth requirement, as a more exacting requirement than the first, but of essentially the same kind. The invoking of the truth requirement makes A reconsider whether the grounds are really adequate. He will reflect, 'Remember: it is a question here of what is the case, not merely belief or conviction; therefore be critical in your examination of the evidence!'

In other words, the effect of introducing the analysis to people engaged in assessing p is to bring pressure to bear upon them to increase the standard of adequacy. And further, if they yield to the pressure the effect will be to distort usage: in the form of the adoption of a terminology with unusually severe requirements for saying 'I know that p' and 'p is true'.

Looking closely, then, at the empirical evidence on how we actually tend to behave in situations in which we are confronted with the three requirements, it seems impossible or highly unnatural to conclude anything in terms of *conceptual constructions* of knowledge. In applying the three requirements we find no neat concept of knowledge such as an analysis in terms of them suggests. The material evidence, in fact, provides no indication of such a set of mutually complementary conditions in cases of the normal use of 'I know that p'.

In so far, then, as a three-requirement analysis expresses a model of reaching towards truth and grasping it in a way in which it is guaranteed, it seems that the model does not apply. The model, or frame of reference, or metaphor of gradually reaching knowledge through increases in evidence simply cannot be adapted to summing up or conceptualizing the empirical material.

If I gradually come nearer and nearer to an apple I can eventually grasp it. This latter event is clearly something very different from merely getting close to the apple. In reaching for something it is possible, for example, to reach too far, in our eagerness or drunkenness. Having grasped it one may lose one's grip. Or one may be forestalled by someone else reaching it first. All this contrasts with our striving or reaching for knowledge. We may in some sense measure an increase in evidence, but we cannot measure the approximations to knowledge where knowledge requires truth. The event of grasping is just not forthcoming and nothing corresponds to reaching beyond, losing one's grip, or being forestalled.

There are, on the other hand, some similarities between reaching knowledge and reaching apples. We may be mistaken in our belief that we have reached the apple. Darkness may make our judgment unreliable, or somebody may have put a wooden 'apple' on the branch in order to teach us philosophy. But the clear and sufficiently relevant difference between reaching an apple and reaching a piece of knowledge lies in the conceptualization of the process. In order to reach the apple one must not only come sufficiently near to it; something entirely new must happen, namely the actual grasping of the apple. And whether we are mistaken or not in believing it is a genuine apple, the actual grasping is conceivable and is conceived as an independent event providing a new kind of experience.

6. CONCLUSION ON 'REACHING' KNOWLEDGE

If we conclude 'Knowledge cannot be reached by increasing the evidence', it sounds as though we were playing into the hands of those who unduly stress human fallibility. But of course the formulation also covers knowledge about failures and errors. No belief can be *known* to be mistaken by increasing the evidence for its negation. So really the formulation indirectly supports infallibility as much as it does fallibility.

The formulation 'knowledge cannot be reached by increasing the evidence' is nevertheless misleading. What we have done is to consider some kinds of sets of proposed necessary and sufficient conditions for 'knowing', especially for the truth of 'I know that *p*'. We have noted that when (*a*) an 'it is the case' requirement, and (*b*) grounds or evidence requirements are made sufficiently precise as separate requirements, there is no process comparable to a reaching and grasping of knowledge by increasing the quality of grounds or evidence. But it is just because there is no such process that the negative, sweepingly general conclusion—compared with the narrowness of the kind of requirements we have considered—may be misleading. It might lead one to think that *reaching* is in any case a good conceptual frame of reference in relation to knowledge, whatever the level of preciseness of the discussion. The empirical material, however, suggests otherwise. It might be less misleading, then, to say 'Knowledge defined conceptually in terms of requirements can neither be reached nor not reached by increasing the evidence', or 'The metaphor of reaching out for, coming gradually nearer, and then eventually grasping is inadequate as a basis for a conceptualization or explication of "knowledge" '.

And even this formulation is not an entirely happy one, since the inadequacy, as far as we have discussed it above, refers to a process of increasing the evidence, which is only one process by which knowledge is obtained. We have not discussed, for example, the possibilities of immediate intuition.

Nevertheless our conclusion has severe repercussions on three-requirement conceptions of knowledge. For it undermines the assumption that there is any basis in how we mostly use 'I know (that so-and-so is the case)' for constructing a concept of knowing which contains both a truth requirement and an evidence requirement, *each of which must be separately fulfilled.*

Now this last qualification might be taken to suggest an alternative solution. If our conceptualization of normal uses of 'I know (that so-and-so is the case)' fails just because it demands that the truth and evidence requirements be separately satisfied, why should we not construct a concept in which the requirements do not require separate answers? That is, why not take the problematic truth requirement to be satisfiable in terms of the unproblematic evidence requirement?

7. CONCEPTS OF KNOWING WITHOUT A SEPARATELY SATISFIED TRUTH REQUIREMENT

In so far as claims to know that so-and-so are typically accepted or rejected on the basis of evidence, either the evidence attributed to the claimant or the evidence the attributer attributes to himself, such a conceptualization might seem to do justice to ordinary usage. But although the proposed conceptualization agrees with ordinary usage in respect of making the evidence requirement the working partner, it departs from ordinary usage in making the truth requirement entirely subordinate to the evidence requirement. What the proposal requires is that we make do with evidence alone, that is, determine knowledge (and thereby truth) exclusively in terms of specified standards of evidence.

Now if the truth requirement and the requirement of adequate evidence are collapsed in this way, it is clear that I can still rationally reconstruct the reaching of knowledge. For if the evidence according to a social standard is less than adequate, then an increase in evidence will eventually make it adequate. There is no special difficulty involved as long as adequacy is defined in relation to specified standards which have already been reached in other cases.[1] Thus, if the presence of an eye-witness is taken as

---

[1] Some will object that the truth requirement is apt to enter anyhow. How do I *know* that a specified standard is fulfilled? If this requires so-and-so to be the case, truth must be reached in the matter. There is no compelling reason, however, why standard evidence should not replace truth here as well, if it can do such a thing at

standard for certain kinds of assertions, the event of getting an eye-witness may at the same time be an event of reaching knowledge. Both events are datable and there is no question of what happens afterwards.

There will even be levels of evidence which more than fulfil the standards, thus making it practicable to localize the lower limit of adequacy between two levels, the level of less than adequate and the level of more than adequate. Then the difficulties of grasping knowledge as a special event as opposed to approximating it naturally disappear.

There are, however, cogent reasons for rejecting definitions in terms of standards of evidence. They lead to paradoxes, or at least to terminological oddities that few would tolerate once they were made aware of them. In other words, this conceptualization of knowledge, just as the previous one, leads to perplexities and to a negative conclusion.

To see how this is so, consider the following tentative equivalences (omitting the 'being sure' requirement for the sake of simplicity):

(1a)[1] A knows now at time t that p—A's evidence now at time t that p, satisfies the standard of evidence valid now at time t in the field to which p belongs

(1b) A knew at time t that p—A's evidence at time t that p, satisfied the standard of evidence valid at time t in the field to which p belongs

(1c) A was mistaken at time t that he knew that p—A's evidence at time t that p, did not satisfy the standard of evidence valid at time t in the field to which p belongs

Now, so long as we retain the conventional idea that standards of evidence are modifiable, the conceptualization of 'I know' in terms of specific standards of evidence will clearly lead to paradoxes. Thus, the left-hand proposition (1a) is not contradicted

[1] It is crucial that (1a), (1b), (1c) are *not* taken to introduce general concepts of 'knows', 'knew', and 'mistaken'. In order to make use of (1a), (1b), (1c) there must by definition be references to an N.N., a *t*, and a *p*, and these references must be part of the conceptualizations.

***

all. There remains the objection that the replacement would lead to an infinite regress. We must have adequate evidence that there is adequate evidence that there is adequate evidence . . . The objection is not a serious one, however, so long as it is not shown that the regress is vicious or fatal.

by the following left-hand propositions of (2a) or (2b) in the case that the equivalence (1a) holds:

(2a) A knows at time $t + 1$ that not-p—A's evidence now at time $t + 1$ that not-p, satisfies the standard of evidence valid now at time $t + 1$, in the field to which p belongs

(2b) B knows now at time t that p—B's evidence now at time t that p, satisfies the standard of evidence valid now at time t in the field to which p belongs

In short, giving up the separate truth requirement results in concepts of knowledge according to which two contradictory propositions may both be known, or in concepts relative to time, situation, person, or materials of evidence.

If, on the other hand, we try to resolve the paradox by avoiding the relativity to person and time, we would have to allow that there could be standards of evidence that rendered mistake impossible. But this would exclude the modification of the relevant standards of evidence. Yet surely if we ask ourselves in what cases we would accept that evidence implied incorrigibility, we would have to allow that even if there were cases, they would seem to be so rare and uninteresting in practical life that using 'know' *only* in those cases would virtually render the term inapplicable.

It should be noted that even if there are statements known for certain to be true, this does not show that the certainty arises from *evidence* making mistake impossible. And incorrigible statements may not even be true, let alone known to be true, since statements might be incorrigibly false.

In any case, in so far as the establishment of social standards of evidence is not a mere fiction, these standards are fixed at levels which can be disputed. Indeed, it is the disputable character of evidence which motivates the institution of standards. Also they function to avoid too severe as well as too lenient requirements of knowing; they do not function to institute the severest possible requirements. The *possibility* of agreeing to the statement 'It was generally accepted that we knew that p, but it was a mistake' is left open.

If we accept

(3) If at least one person knows that p, then p is known.

Then, if (1a) and (2b) are true we accept as possible

(4) Both p and not-p are known.

In general, the following constellations among others are possible if A and B are two different persons:

A knows that p, B knows that not-p.
A knew that p, A knows that not-p.
A knew that p, B knew that not-p.

The possibility is not to be qualified as *remote*, for even in scientific textbooks a considerable percentage of statements judged to express knowledge are retracted as time passes. Applying (3) we get a mass of combinations of the following kinds.

Now p is known, while earlier not-p was known.
Now p is known in the scientific community A, whereas not-p is known in B.

In case standards in a field are successively increased in severity from level L_1 to L_2, and from L_2 to L_3, etc., 'known' would have to be indexed:

Now p is L_3-known (and therefore also L_2- and L_1-known), while earlier not-p was L_2-known.
In the backward (?) community A, not-p is L_1-known, in B, p is L_2-known, in C, L_3-known.

The contradiction or inconsistency can of course be avoided if we drop the notion 'known' and adopt evidence-concepts: 'N.N. had at time t standard evidence', etc. But although the more complex notion does not lead to contradictions, neither, unfortunately, does it solve the problems connected with 'knowing'.

Note that the equivalences (1a)–(1c) make it necessary to retract the statement that p is known by N.N. only if certain historical investigations concerning *standards* lead to results that differ from previous ones. *New evidence directly concerning p is irrelevant.* It cannot change the verdict 'N.N. knows that p', because it relates to the present and cannot affect 'N.N. knew that p'. Whatever the amount of evidence amassed in the future in support of not-p, the proposition 'N.N. knew at time t that p' will be true. However, evidence that N.N. after all did not have the socially required evidence may result in a denial that N.N. knew.

One of the negations of (1a) and (1c) runs as follows:

(5a) A does not know now at time t that p—A's evidence now at time t that p, does not satisfy the standard . . .

(5c) A was not mistaken at time t that he knew that p—A's evidence at time t that p, *did* satisfy the standard . . .

And more complex statements:

(6) A knows that C's evidence at time t that p did satisfy the standards, but B knew that it did not.

(7) A has standard evidence that C's evidence that p was up to standard, but B had standard evidence that C's evidence that p was not up to standard.

Consider guns. There are certain manipulations which once performed justify one in saying 'The gun is unloaded', but, of course, very strange circumstances may occur such that one may later establish adequate evidence that it was in fact loaded. If N.N. had adequate evidence at one o'clock that the gun was *unloaded* but had adequate evidence at two o'clock that it was loaded at one o'clock, he still *knew* at one o'clock that it was unloaded. In court he may say 'Yes, the gun killed the dog at about one o'clock. From that time I knew it was loaded, but just before that I knew it was not loaded. Because I knew it was unloaded, I have no responsibility for what happened to the dog. I agree the gun *was* loaded all the time, but for part of the time I *knew* it was *not*'.

If knowing is defined in terms of satisfaction of definite standards of evidence, *however high*, and one keeps the definition in mind—eradicating any association of knowing with truth and being-the-case—such pieces of conversation as the following could occur:

'Several people knew he was the murderer, but of course, as you know, he was not. Among those who knew he was the murderer, there are still some who think they know. The rest know he was not, they knew only until last spring.'

Or:

'A is right in maintaining that the spectrobolometric method as used by Astronomer B satisfies our standard of evidence, and that the radar method as used by astronomer C does so also. B found that the distance to the sun is smaller than k, C found it is greater than k. In other words, B knew it was smaller, C that it was greater. It is therefore correct to claim, as *A* does, that in view of *B*'s and *C*'s results, we know both that the distance is greater and that it is smaller.'

Finally, there would be extreme oddity in the account given of scientific research. The scientist would continually be finding himself encumbered with truths which his later researches would strongly incline him to renounce. Rather than have so much conflicting, even contradictory, knowledge on his hands his wisest course might be to consign all rejected theories to a closed file marked 'knowledge', and be content to concentrate henceforth on untruths. Or perhaps the natural result, both in scientific and everyday matters, would be a kind of despairing reappraisal of all past efforts and a sceptical pronouncement that none of the evidence obtained so far was correctly taken to guarantee, or to be tantamount to, the truth. The file marked 'knowledge' would then have to be emptied.

So much, then, for the bold decision to conceptualize knowledge and truth in terms solely of evidence. If carried out, the use of the term 'know' would differ so much from most usages relating to 'know that *p*' as to be grossly misleading. If knowing is to be equated with having evidence of some kind, it would be better not to use the term 'know' but to speak simply of having evidence of this or that particular kind, or simply of having standard or adequate evidence.

The conceptualizations of 'It is probable that *p*' are mainly in terms of evidence. Attempts to conceptualize 'I know that *p*' in terms of 'It is very probable that *p*' therefore do not avoid the possibilities of both *p* and not-*p* being known. Lack of space forbids our going into details concerning the complexities of probability constructs.

8. SUGGESTION NOT TO USE KNOWLEDGE EXPRESSIONS UNDER CERTAIN CIRCUMSTANCES

In the foregoing I have argued that to require truth and evidence as two clearly separate, precise requirements of knowledge leads to the conclusion that we can never *reach* knowledge by an increase in evidence. If, on the other hand, we leave out truth as a distinct requirement and limit ourselves to requiring standard evidence, we get a strange use of 'to know' and might as well eliminate the truth in favour of the evidence terminology, or, even better, in favour of a combined statement of degree and kind of conviction or belief and status of evidence (grounds included).[1]

What we can validly conclude at this point must be carefully distinguished. All we have indicated is that it is difficult to make sense of the idea of attaining to knowledge on the basis solely of evidence, where the transition from not-yet-knowing to knowing is marked by some identifiable event. There are two consequences that it is important to note do not follow from this conclusion. First, it does not follow that we do not or cannot know anything or even that it is less probable that we know anything. The difficulty we have discussed is that of identifying any event as the transitional point at which a mere belief becomes a true belief or where a true belief becomes a belief known to be true. From this we can conclude at most that we cannot conceptualize our use of expressions of the form 'I know that p' when we intend them to convey information about such an event. But of course it is doubtful whether the impossibility of identifying such an event means that an event of the kind in question cannot occur. At least this would require other, debatable, premises. Therefore not only does the possibility of our having knowledge remain open, in terms of the above discussion, but also the possibility of our arriving at or coming *somehow* to knowledge. What is excluded is that we can conceptualize and point to an event which we know constitutes our arrival at knowledge.

The second main consequence that does *not* follow from the conclusion of our discussion is that expressions of the form 'I know that p', and other knowledge expressions, cannot be used in their normal sense for purposes of satisfactory communication.

As I shall try to show, the ordinary and normal use of such expressions does not require that the event of reaching knowledge be clearly distinguished from that of acquiring certain standard or accepted evidence. Nor does it require that it *not* be so distinguished. Such requirements are parts of explicit conceptualizations. It is only when knowledge expressions are used to express these conceptualizations that any difficulties arising out of the requirements affect their utility or smooth functioning.

[1] This would be better considering the frequent occurrence of an extremely high degree of evidence in relation to standards nevertheless combined with disbelief. Scientists with strong intuitions have been led to important discoveries through mistrusting evidence that has more than fulfilled the requirements of the scientific community—and they have sometimes stuck to a theory that has prestige in spite of counterevidence that seems completely compelling to later generations.

In the great majority of cases explicit conceptualizations do not enter into, and thus do not determine, our use of such expressions. With regard to 'I know that p', in cases where the requirements of evidence and truth are not explicitly made, therefore, I suggest that the use of knowledge expressions is unproblematic. Thus what I propose is that one may persist in using the terms 'know' and 'knowledge', but only in situations where it is taken for granted by the language community, or at least by the persons I speak to, that I do not make definite *conceptual requirements* concerning what is implied by something being known.

In seeking to justify the decision to persist in using the terms, therefore, I point to the term 'know' as a term of everyday use that is applied with a certain lack of definiteness or depth of intention in relation to any conceptual framework. This lack of definiteness of intention, so I shall argue, is such that although in their everyday use of knowledge expressions people implicitly acknowledge that what is false cannot be known (for example, when they come to believe that not-p they withdraw any previous claim to know that p), they do not go so far as to *affirm* that what is known cannot be false or that it can. And it is because they do not think through the implication that they are able to envisage identifiable events that constitute not merely the addition of further evidence but the arrival at the truth of the matter itself. When we talk about the truth requirement, therefore, as far as ordinary use goes, neither the affirmation that what I know *cannot* be false nor the affirmation that it *can* will be to the point. They are both beyond what I can be presumed in everyday life to have thought about and to be able to understand and articulate. Thus, my usage will be a function of the definiteness of intention normal in the kind of context in which I use the terms 'know' and 'knowledge'.

It seems that the above considerations impose distinct limitations on the applicability of knowledge expressions, limitations which concern the use we have for the distinction between knowing that so-and-so and not knowing that so-and-so. We can put this more explicitly by saying that the considerations limit the range of situations in which an affirmation that we do have knowledge or an affirmation that we do not have it functions informatively. To conclude that in such situations the distinction is reasonably withheld would be to argue for suspension of judgment, and in what follows I shall argue for the decision to abstain from trying to *use the distinction* between knowing and not-knowing in three, in part overlapping, kinds of situations. This amounts to a rejection of any Yes or No answers to the question 'Can knowledge be reached?'

First, though we *affirm*, for instance, the principle of contradiction, we nevertheless delimit the scope of the distinction in such a way that it does not make sense to state that the principle furnishes an instance of knowledge or of lack of knowledge.[1]

Aristotle himself argued against the application of the term 'knowledge' (*epistémé*) to first principles (*archai*). The principle of contradiction does not rest on evidence, he contends, because to accept a proposition on the basis of evidence already presupposes that the principle of contradiction is true. And since one cannot be said to know something without implying that one can point to evidence, the principle of contradiction is not an instance of knowledge. In saying that one does not and cannot *know* any principle, however, Aristotle did not imply that we are not in possession of its truth. He seems rather to have meant to reject not only the status of knowledge but also the *distinction* between known and unknown with regard to the principles.

Today Aristotle would have some support in contending that we possess certain truths without evidence, but there are also strong movements in favour of looking at such 'truth' as presuppositions, postulates, basic assumptions which are neither true nor false. (This would be my position, but it will not be relevant in arguments put forward here.)

Then, secondly, there is the situation of scientific research. The rules or principles of research methodology are such that at no point is the evidence for a proposition (if there is evidence for it at all) such that it cannot be increased. The rules themselves point out the ways of increase. The weight of a piece of evidence, for instance, a document containing the report of a set of observations, inevitably decreases with time—after a sufficiently long time it comes into the hands of critical historians who apply their own

---

[1] In my article 'Can Knowledge be Reached?' (*Inquiry*, Vol. 4 [1961], No. 4) I did not sufficiently stress the difference between, on the one hand, considering the distinction between knowing and not knowing to be inapplicable or inappropriate in certain situations and, on the other, denying that knowledge (in certain senses) can be reached. As a consequence of this, I considered the negative answer to the question in the title automatically to *comprise* a kind of scepticism. It is more accurate to say that it may be used to support sceptical conclusions, but only if other premises are added.

cold rules for assessing the weight of written sources. As long as this development is kept in mind, there is no occasion, except in popularizations, for using the knowledge and truth terminology.

The basic methodological model in conceptualizing the relation between a proposition of research and its reference is such that there is no necessary connection between evidence and reference: whatever the evidence, the proposition may or may not be true. The status of evidence is in principle irrelevant because it is constantly shifting, whereas the proposition is either true or false all the time. If there is any kind of implied sceptical bent in this, and I think there is, then it is one that cannot appropriately be formulated in terms of knowing. For reasons already stated, to say that knowledge *cannot* be *reached* would be misleading. The terminology of evidence, confirmation, and corroboration is fitted to the model of unending research.

Although one may speak of a community of researchers, it is not of the kind in which one researcher '*vouches* for the truth' (Ayer[1]) of what he or others say. Vouching, swearing, promising, or pledging one's honour have no place in scientific methodology. The term 'scientific knowledge' is widely used among researchers when talking about comprehensive sets of sentences, but in the more professionally serious and heavily conceptualized parts of their articles and books 'I know that so-and-so' and related phrases are rare. There is little importance attached to considerations about which propositions have and which do not have the status of knowledge. Thus, to refrain from using knowledge expressions in scientific texts does not create any problems affecting research communications, and is a common practice.

9. USE OF 'KNOW' AND DEFINITENESS OF INTENTION

We have mentioned as an explanation of the fact that vernacular distinctions between what is and what is not known and between knowledge reached and knowledge not reached do not always work, a factor which we have termed 'definiteness of intention'.[2]

The general idea of degrees of definiteness of intention is as follows. When, under definite circumstances at a definite date, I

---

[1] 'To say that I know . . . is not so much to report my state of mind as to vouch for the truth of whatever it may be' (*The Problem of Knowledge*, p. 17).

[2] The concept is introduced in my *Interpretation and Preciseness* (2nd edn. forthcoming, Bedminster Press, New York), pp. 77 ff.

use a sentence (or, more generally, an expression) to express something, I intend just this something and nothing else. Reflection, perhaps provoked by questions I myself or others pose, may however show or suggest indefiniteness in the form of vagueness or otherwise respecting the borders between the intended something and other things.

Certain distinctions may or may not have been present to my mind, or have been present with varying degrees of clearness. Or, although introspection does not reveal any such conscious distinguishing, nevertheless subsequent events both of a verbal and a non-verbal kind may allow us to posit that the distinctions were used. They were available or present-able to my consciousness even if they were not in it ('prebewusst' or 'preconscious' in the terminology of Freud).

Using an expression like 'I know that so-and-so', it *may* be present to my mind or at least present-able that certain requirements (for instance, honesty, correct grammar) are (or are not) fulfilled. The definiteness of intention *in the direction* of one kind of requirement, for instance, concerning the distinction between true and false, may be sharp, but in other directions, say, concerning the distinction between truth and evidence, it may be small. In that case, although I may be able to report that in saying 'I know that so-and-so' I implied that so-and-so is *true*, the question of truth may not have been present to my mind as a separate question from that of evidence. Confronted with the question of the quality of my evidence, I may report honestly that in saying I knew, I intended to require good or sufficient evidence and found the requirement satisfied, but I did not make a distinction between that and truth. Or else I find that to some extent I made a distinction and took it for granted that with such good evidence, truth was guaranteed, or just there as a corollary. A great variety of other kinds of reports may be had from persons (professors of philosophy and others) trying to find out what they intended when they said they knew so-and-so.

Measurements of definiteness of intention can be surveyed by maps showing various directions of what can be termed 'precization'. If T_0 is a sentence, say, 'I know that Columbus discovered America in 1492', more precise sentences (which are not interpretations of each other), let us call them T_1, T_2, . . ., represent main directions of precization. Sentences still more precise than T_1 may be symbolized by $T_{1.1}$, $T_{1.2}$, . . . The limit of the definiteness of intention of a person who has uttered T_0 is indicated by reporting which sentence is just within and which sentence is just beyond the discrimination of that person. Thus, one person may have intended something in the direction of T_2 (rather than T_1, T_3, . . .), but did not take into account the differences between T_2 . $_1$, T_2 . $_2$, etc. Another may have intended T_2 . $_2$, but did not have sufficient definiteness of intention to discriminate between T_2 . $_2$. $_1$, T_2 . $_2$. $_2$, etc. He neither meant to express T_2 . $_2$. $_1$ nor *not* to express T_2 . $_2$. $_1$. They are transintentional.

Let us now apply this apparatus to

(1) T_0—I know that p

As first-order precizations we could take some of the different conceptualizations in terms of three requirements. But we should also take some other formulations, as follows:

$$T_0 \text{ I know that } p \begin{cases} T_1 \begin{cases} \text{I am convinced that } p \text{ and} \\ \text{I have adequate evidence that } p \text{ and} \\ p \text{ is true} \end{cases} \\ T_2 \begin{cases} \text{I believe that } p \text{ and} \\ p \text{ is true} \end{cases} \\ T_3 \text{ I have adequate evidence that } p \\ T_4 \text{ I have verified that } p \\ T_5 \text{ I am willing to vouch for } p \end{cases}$$

Many people have a definiteness of intention that is insufficient to discriminate even these first-order precizations. (They may show very sensitive discriminations, but not in exactly the directions listed.)

In order to explore the limits of the definiteness of intention among those who intended something like T_1 by T_0 a selection of second-order precizations must be used. They can be constructed on the basis of the following two sets of precizations of certain parts of T_1 and by precizations of a third sentence W_0:

$$U_0 \text{ I have adequate evidence that } p \begin{cases} U_1 \text{ I have evidence satisfying the social standard valid for the field to which } p \text{ belongs, and justifying my saying } p \text{ is true} \\ U_2 \text{ I have such good evidence that it is unreasonable to doubt that } p \text{ is true} \\ U_3 \text{ I have conclusive evidence that } p \end{cases}$$

V_0 p is true
$$\begin{cases} V_1 \text{ there is conclusive evidence that } p \\ V_2 \text{ it is the case that } p \\ V_3 \text{ } p \text{ belongs to an all-embracing co-} \\ \text{herent system} \end{cases}$$

W_0 If U_0, then V_0

One of the precizations of U_0 is in all relevant respects identical with one of the precizations of V_0. For those who by U_0 intend U_3 and by V_0 intend V_1 there is no special difficulty in answering both questions, 'Do you have adequate evidence?' and 'Is p true?' They take the questions to mean the same.

The other combinations (U_i, V_j) may be put in two classes: those for whom a positive answer to U_0 *somehow* implies a positive answer to V_0, and those for whom V_0 is an entirely new proposition.

For those who allow V_0 somehow to be implied by U_0, a set of precizations of W_0: If U_0, then V_0, is worked out. Its function is to elicit reactions showing exactly how individual persons think U_0 is connected with V_0.

The working hypotheses based on preliminary empirical findings are as follows:

1. Most people have a definiteness of intention using 'I know that p', and closely related sentences, which falls short of $T_1, T_2, \ldots$

2. Very few have a definiteness of intention sufficient to discriminate $T_1 . _1, T_1 . _2, \ldots$

3. The smooth application of 'I know that p' is hindered as soon as the precizations $T_1, T_2, \ldots$ are applied, and very strongly inhibited if $T_1 . _1, T_1 . _2, \ldots$ are applied.

4. Those who intend something definite in relation to first- or second-order precizations have difficulties in being consistent.

In this last hypothesis I refer to reactions to questions relating to evidence gathered by A supporting p and by B supporting not-p. People get into trouble when made aware of the possibilities of contradictions.

The general conclusion to be drawn is this: the use of 'I know that p' has limited applicability; it cannot be mapped out in relation to a set of precise concepts. It works as long as such relations are ignored.

One of the reasons why it is rather difficult to keep variations in definiteness of intention in mind is that these differences are not usually indicated by separate words or phrases. To use such phrases as 'loosely speaking', 'vaguely suggested', 'with not too great an emphasis on unambiguousness' would help very little and could make texts unreadable, or at least unread.

The first sentence of Section 4 is a case in point. Three 'things' are 'required', and the requirement is then formulated in very loose words, considering the complexity of the subject. The first requirement, that one must be sure, is suggested by the vague words 'one must be sure'. Some people tend to interpret these words in the direction of an actually felt, strong conviction. But in that case very many instances of 'know' would be misuses, because claims to know are by no means always accompanied by any such strong feelings. Especially in the case of textbooks, or of a lecturer repeating certain statements for the tenth time, the only feeling to be experienced is likely to be one of boredom.

So there is a *variety of requirements* which might all be loosely expressed by 'one must be sure'. Indeed, the phrase may not be so bad as an initial formulation, chosen *because of*, not in spite of, its indefiniteness, as is precisely the case in Section 4, where in order not to close the doors to a number of interesting and relevant requirements the formulations are purposefully kept vague.

But there is something more important to be remembered. Saying, as I have just done, that there is a variety of requirements which might all be loosely expressed by 'one must be sure' (T_0), it is suggested that by taking a step towards clarification I could propose at least two formulations (T_1 and T_2) which in a simple, unambiguous way express two definite requirements, R_1 and R_2. Implicit in this suggestion is that I have two such requirements 'in mind', that they exist already, and that the only question is how to express them.

The principle of limitation and relativity of definiteness, however, goes against this simplistic view of the situation. In order to bring out the full consequences of this principle, we need to substitute for the concept of precization that of direction of precization.

If T_1 and T_2 are two precizations of T_0, and $T_{1.1}$ and $T_{2.1}$ are two precizations of T_1 and T_2, two main directions of precization are indicated: that from T_0 through T_1 and that from T_0 through T_2. There is in theory no halting place or end, but it is convenient to talk *as if* there were: we say that 'to be sure' may mean this or that, mentioning two precizations. These are taken as expressive of two concepts of being sure. But it would be better to talk of concepts in the direction of so-and-so and concepts in other directions, taking precizations as indicators of directions.

Applying this to what we have been calling 'requirements', we may now talk of sets of three requirements, each *ad hoc* delimited by three expressions, namely those used in the opening passage of Section 4. That is, those expressions are used as initial formulations (T_0, U_0, V_0).

The question Do everyday uses of 'I know that p' satisfy the three requirements may now be restated so as to avoid an important impasse:

Do everyday uses of 'I know that p' satisfy the three requirements at least at one level of definiteness of intention, and if so, at what level?

This new way of putting the question does not exclude the possibility that one answers Yes in relation to certain levels and No in relation to others.

From the new point of view it is also clear that to speak straightforwardly about requirements is only justifiable in a very tentative manner: it may be that to people in a particular discussion no definite requirements are intended, in the sense that all the participants may have deliberately limited their definiteness of intention.

What is intended when an expression like 'I know that p' is used in everyday situations *is mostly and on the whole not definite enough* in relation to questions of evidence and truth to warrant any explication *or* precization in terms of definite sets of precise requirements involving conceptualizations of 'evidence' and 'truth'. All such sets of requirements will therefore represent transintentional entities—entities going beyond, but not necessarily against, the intention of the speaker, writer, or listener. If transintentional precizations of 'I know that p' pointed in one main direction, furnishing consistent concepts of knowledge, it might not be highly problematic to use 'I know that p' in situations in which it is necessary to show great care concerning the status of p. But epistemological discussion shows that vast difficulties have to be surmounted in order to find even one consistent trans- (but not anti-) intentional concept. The most reasonable policy is therefore to avoid the expression 'I know that p' in situations where a considerable definiteness of intention is required concerning that status of p.

The third kind of situation in which the use of the terms 'know', 'knowing', 'knowledge', etc., are not to be recommended can therefore be described as the kind of situation in which a definiteness of intention in epistemic matters is required that goes beyond that of everyday situations. By epistemic matters I refer to questions concerning certainty, evidence, and probability. Thus formulated the third kind of situation may include instances of the two foregoing.

Expressions of the form 'I know that p' lead to satisfactory communication if the required definiteness is low. The expressions 'I have adequate evidence that p' and 'p is true' function satisfactorily if used separately. *What does not succeed is to explicate the first in terms of the last two.*

It does not succeed because, as we have seen, conceptual clarification of the terms involved makes it impossible to apply the metaphor of reaching truth when establishing truth is taken as a separate concept from acquiring adequate evidence. And if it is not taken as separate the consequence will be that contradictory propositions can both be known. (Thus 'I know that p and he knows that not-p'.)

Increased definiteness of intention shows itself in the application of a more discriminating set of distinctions. The third kind of situation might therefore also be described as situations in which a set of precise distinctions is presumed to be applied which is foreign to or inconsistent with the vernacular use of 'know', 'knowing', etc. The notion of definiteness of intention is useful in order to make clear what kind of inconsistency is relevant here.

10. CONCLUSION ON THE COMPLEMENTARITY OF TRUTH AND EVIDENCE

That under certain conditions a set of distinctions implied by knowledge expressions cannot be usefully applied is sufficient basis for a recommendation that the corresponding affirmations 'I know' and 'I do not know' be withheld where these conditions obtain. Under these conditions, then, it is reasonable to withhold judgment. According to the arguments, the only cases where the conditions preventing applicability do not obtain are those where knowledge expressions are used with limited depth of intention, in fact where they function not to convey clear and precise distinctions but as more or less conceptually innocent gestures, something approaching the 'utterances' or 'sounds' (*fonai*) mentioned by Sextus Empiricus[1] in connection with the sceptic's avoidance of doctrinally contaminated ways of expression. Thus the force of our discussion on the complementarity of truth and evidence is such as to bring out the strength of Pyrrhonian scepticism as described by Sextus. The awkwardness of applying knowledge expressions when they are intended to convey in any precise manner the distinction between truth and evidence makes suspension of judgment at the corresponding depth of intention reasonable. Where the depth of intention is such that 'I know that p' implies complementarily that p is true and that I have evidence for p, the affirmation expressed by 'I know that p' no longer has the applicability which the same expression has when the truth and evidence requirements are not intended as complementary. Thus the applicability of a claim to know that so-and-so is a function of depth, or definiteness, of intention.

Where depth of intention precludes the application of a knowledge expression it does not, of course, follow that the statement expressed by it would be false. Our conclusion that in certain circumstances the application of knowledge expressions becomes awkward is not to be taken to justify a general negative conclusion about the possibility of knowledge, nor even about the difficulty of acquiring knowledge in these circumstances.

Nor are we to infer that because the application of knowledge expressions depends on certain distinctions not being made precise these expressions 'really' have no application, that their only possible use amounts to misuse. What has been pointed out is only that there are good reasons for not using knowledge expressions in certain circumstances, the circumstances in question being those in which the truth and evidence requirements of knowledge are conceptually distinguished. It is not implied that because in the vernacular use of these expressions there is a failure to think this distinction through, such use is in some sense debased. The inapplicability or awkwardness of a vernacular term in certain kinds of situations should not be taken to indicate an imperfection in the vernacular, but as a warning that the limits of the area of useful application of certain terms are sometimes closer at hand than one might expect.

[1] See p. 8, above.

V

DIALECTICS OF MODERN
EPISTEMOLOGICAL SCEPTICISM

I. INTRODUCTION

A GOOD deal of discussion about knowledge nowadays incorporates arguments attributed to 'the sceptic'. But as we have seen, this figure is a very different man from the sceptic outlined by Sextus Empiricus. Typically scepticism is treated as a position which, if true, would be fatal for any attempted *philosophical* justification of ordinary notions of everyday or scientific knowledge. In fact it might not be inaccurate to say that the position has been generated out of the very attempt to provide such a justification; at any rate, the significance of the modern sceptic's arguments lies precisely in their power to demonstrate that no such attempt can succeed. Sextus Empiricus would label those who hold such a position Academicians, people who hold an absolutist kind of view which he clearly distinguishes from the 'way' of the sceptic.

The modern sceptic, or epistemological sceptic, is made to *argue* that knowledge is impossible, to *insist* that we cannot know anything, to *affirm* that it is true or can be known that knowledge is not possible.[1] Naturally enough, although this sceptic's arguments are taken seriously and some steps in them even accepted,[2] the position they support is not one that any flesh-and-blood philosopher is anxious to occupy; indeed, to be forced to do so would most likely be seen as a professional defeat by those who look upon the philosopher's task as that of explaining, rather than replacing, well-established everyday beliefs. It is because the sceptic's reasoning is considered intuitively false and yet logically

---

[1] We should recall that some of the phrases (*fonai*) which Sextus calls sceptical do not, when uttered by sceptics, express any doctrine or view whatsoever.

[2] Cf. especially Bertrand Russell in *Human Knowledge* and A. J. Ayer in *The Problem of Knowledge*.

impeccable that 'his' arguments are subjected to close and careful epistemological scrutiny.

Two features of modern accounts of scepticism are significant to our discussion, their avoidance of contextual considerations and the elaborate terminology and conceptual structures in which the arguments are framed. A typical procedure is to consider with regard to some statement whether there are sources of error such that later events might cause one to retract a claim that the statement is true. If not, then the statement is 'incorrigible' and we have no right to persist in refusing to affirm its truth on the grounds that it might be false. If there are conceivable sources of error, then the statement is 'corrigible' and we are faced with the problem of whether or not we can 'legitimately' claim to know that it is true.

To cope with this problem a number of concepts are then introduced and developed. The effect of this is that the question of whether it is correct to use expressions of the form and normal intent of 'I know that p' becomes a matter to be dealt with within an elaborate conceptual framework. The assumption is that such frameworks provide the terms in which a *general* question of justifying knowledge claims is to be answered. This general question is then treated as something over and above the question of particular contextual justifications for the use of expressions ('Should I have said "thank you"?'). The epistemologist presumes his conclusions to apply in all contexts. Although he acknowledges that for all practical purposes there is no need to refer to his arguments, he thinks of them as showing us what 'strictly' we can or cannot say. The assumption seems to be that any well-equipped society catering to the enlightened interest of its members would make philosophical conclusions about knowledge publicly available, perhaps in reference libraries, or better, as an addition to the telephone service so that people could at any time or in any situation or stage of debate be given the authoritative view on the matter. (We might sympathize with the unfortunate man entrusted with the task of compiling such conclusions. Faced with arguments, authoritative and apparently technically proficient, to the effect that 'material object' statements are/are not conclusively verifiable, that perception is a direct/indirect relation, and if indirect that 'perception' statements then can/cannot be known with certainty to be true (or false), that in making such statements we make/do not make inferences which, if we are to justify the claim to know such statements to be true must be/need not be valid inferences, and so on, he would almost certainly recommend suspension of judgment in his letter of resignation. Strictly speaking, of course, any headway he made would only add to the confusion.)

To deny that there were general questions about the applicability of knowledge expressions besides the considerations of context would be fruitless. It is a matter of fact that people ask them. But when they are asked and answered in terms of explicit conceptual frameworks that have no part in ordinary usage the relevance of the answers to ordinary knowledge claims becomes problematic.

The problem can be posed as the question whether epistemology concerns knowledge claims in general, or knowledge claims only as they are understood by epistemologists, that is, in their own special frameworks. If the former, then we must suppose that the typical epistemological conclusion, for example, that knowledge claims about material objects cannot be justified, leaves the ordinary kinds of justification intact. The latter are all right in their place, and it is not for the epistemologist to question, say, the standards accepted among bird-watchers or people who want to know the time. He does not wish to pose as a more conscientious bird-watcher and time-teller; nor does the epistemological sceptic conclude that no bird-watching or time-telling can be conscientious enough. Rather, he questions whether the standards accepted by bird-watchers and time-tellers amount to valid inferences, whether they allow us to bridge 'logical gaps', and so on. The question of justification, therefore, is one that he takes up at a quite different level and in a terminology quite alien to that of the average, or even exceptionally scrupulous, bird-watcher or time-teller. His attitude, in fact, is parallel to that attributed to the sceptic when, as we noted in an earlier chapter, he is said to arrive at a *modus vivendi* by accepting that it is one thing to live (to watch birds and tell the time) and another to philosophize (to make valid inferences and legitimate claims). There, however, we pointed out that since the Pyrrhonian sceptic accepts no philosophical framework, this *modus vivendi* is not available to him. In effect, a justification of Pyrrhonism is based on the fact that he can respond to his surroundings verbally, and in other ways, in a manner that does not require a corresponding response to propositions. Thus he is not compelled to adopt two minds towards a proposition, one practical and the other theoretical. The propositions he is asked to accept on the basis of his experiences have a depth of intention that bears no comparison with that of his own straightforward acknowledgments of the appearances. This suggests a totally different view of the significance of epistemological discussion, and it is this view, the second alternative, that we shall explore in the following. We shall look at philosophical discussions of knowledge as linear extensions, a kind of tenacious continuation, of ordinary dialogues with a stress on explicit frameworks that is not found in the initial stages. Instead of regarding the epistemologist as an *ex officio* member of the community we shall see him as a participant in a comparatively rare kind of dialogue with a stress on explicit frameworks. The effect will be to present his conclusions, in particular sceptical conclusions such as 'Nothing can be known' and 'No statement can be known to be true', as statements in need of severe qualifications.

2. STANDARDS RELATIVE TO STAGE OF DIALOGUE

Our main task will be to explore, first, the kind of debate or sets of verbal exchanges that foster or tend to foster (modern) scepticism, and secondly, the possibilities of rationally reconstructing such a tendency. This line is adopted because it seems to me that despite the wide acceptance of the view that we ought, as philosophers, to appeal to particular situations or occasions, there has been a sad and significant neglect of one kind of situation, namely that which occurs as a link in a long chain of discussion. Such links, and the chains they form part of, bring out an important aspect of the use of language which can do much to illuminate the dialectics of modern scepticism.

Philosophically the most familiar kind of verbal chain of discussion is the dialogue, and the points I would like to elaborate here arise from simple considerations of the way in which, after three or four exchanges of views in a dialogue, an expression like 'I know' can come to be used in a number of quite different ways.[1]

[1] In the following the phrase 'I know' is fairly consistently adhered to instead of the long series of phrases 'I know', 'He knows', 'I knew', 'He knew', 'knowledge', 'It is known', etc. Having made up one's mind about functions and use of 'I know', the conclusions on the other phrases are in the main predetermined. But only in the main. If one wishes to talk about all the expressions of the series, there turns out to be very little to say. However, there are so many differences to be noted that a painstaking exposition concerned with all these phrases would be rather confusing.

More particularly a use of 'I know that p' at the opening of the debate may be very different from an 'I know that p' repeated after a long argument for and against p. The claim to know at the opening of the dialogue could be an innocent off-hand gesture compared with a coolly insistent stand in the face of arguments and after deliberations, perhaps also certain non-verbal inquiries. It is because of this stress on developing dialogues that I call my notes on modern scepticism dialectical. Perhaps I should apologize to Hegelians for this old, but not very profound or Hegelian, use of the word, and to Austinians for employing such a pretentiously solemn one.

Consider first this example of a simple dialogue and its consequences for the use of 'I know':

(1) A: Do you know where Mr. Jones lives?

(2) B: Certainly, I know. 12 Park Avenue.

(3) A: Letters to him written to that address are returned by the post office.

(4) B: Is that so?

(5) C: Do you know where Mrs. Jones lives?

(6) B: Mm, I was sure 12 Park Avenue was correct. But after what you said—I'm not so certain.

(7) C: Do you know the address of *any* of the people we are going to invite?

(8) B: I'm sure about some of them.

(9) C: Well, this is of deadly importance. Do you actually *know* any of those addresses?

(10) B: I dare say I do know.

But now if at step (10) of the dialogue B persists in using the term 'know', he is likely to have used more rigorous requirements of evidence than at (1). He is also likely to answer with higher definiteness of intention as regards both relevance of evidence and gap (or difference) between evidence and the evidenced. Or, to put it more simply, he sees the need of evidence as he is made more aware of the divergence between his contentions and the evidence he has for them.

This shows that what an individual finds reasonable to require of an 'I know that p' claim will show variation as we move along the steps of a dialogue. Moreover, any such variation might well be classified as 'reasonable', since there seems no reason why we should describe standards of evidence which remain constant as reasonable or normal and take the fluctuations in particular cases as deviations from a stable norm.

Consider, for example, how three people, *A*, *B*, and *C*, might embark upon the complicated project of giving a fairly large party. 'Knowing where somebody lives' may after some (normally) heated dialogues rank high in regard to required *standard* of evidence, that is, in what *A*, *B*, and *C* accept as *adequate* evidence—higher, maybe, if such a comparison could be given a good meaning,[1] than the overworked chemist requires when asking his assistant (at the beginning of a dialogue): 'Is the stuff to my right or the stuff to my left triamidotriphenylcarbinol? Do *you* know?' The everyday and the scientific are not clearly separated, nor the philosophical and unphilosophical as to level of requirements. Variation in stage of development in any (normal) interaction between persons can show marked (yet normal) fluctuation in standard of evidence.

In order to avert a premature suspicion that in talking of variation in terms of increase in requirements I wish to push readers in the direction of scepticism, let me stress that at the end of a dialogue requirements may very well drop. Suppose *C* is to be the financial supervisor of the party, and that he tends to say 'I do *not* know the price, I shall have to check it and you must help me'. If *A* and *B* discover that what *C* labels his 'wild guesses' are correct to the penny, there will be recriminations: 'You *say* you don't know, but you know very well.' *C* has to bring his requirements down a step; his environment will legitimately put pressure on him in that direction. He has been overcautious and hampered the preparations for the party.[2]

Thus, either a lowering or an increase of standards may be the so-called 'normal' after certain phases of a dialogue. Instead of the 'normal', however, I would prefer to talk here of the 'rational',

---

[1] The comparison of relative severity of requirements across different situations or topics is extremely difficult. It would seem that the attempt to make such a comparison must lead to the construction of conceptual frameworks of methodology. However interesting in themselves, these throw little light on everyday (or even scientific) evaluation and comparison of standards. The whole idea of definite standards is, of course, to some extent an artificial creation; there is little basis in the everyday use of 'I know' for that fiction—however useful it is in the debate on scepticism.

[2] In this example an individual modifies his requirements. In other cases the group or community does. The use of 'I know he does not cheat' is perhaps less restricted in Middletown because 'it is now years since those shocking revelations—well, you remember'.

that is, of standards being decreased or increased for good practical reasons.

3. MAXIMUM REQUIREMENTS

It is natural that increases in requirements will be talked about in terms of how to *avoid* mistakes, how to *guarantee* truth, how to eliminate *every* source of error. But of course all these strong terms must be taken with a grain of salt. In practice, *far-fetched* sources of error, such as earthquakes in regions where for a long time there have been none, will be frowned upon as motives for changes in requirements. Although 'every source' *means* every source, one must not be fanatical about it; one may, reluctantly or impatiently, acknowledge possibilities of error, yet dismiss them with an easy mind as of no significance.

In short, there is in everyday life always a non-conceptual frame of reference determined by practical purposes, responsibilities, and so on. A dialogue, however, may sometimes concentrate more and more on a conceptual frame, on a system of significations, and then every source may be taken in an absolute sense, that is to say, *every* source.

Once this sense is given and assumed it may then appear preposterous and ridiculous to ask for a guarantee of the elimination of every source of error, but the idea is still one that can be understood. That is, I can say 'I see what you mean, but to require that *every* source be eliminated is of course to require the impossible. Who has ever asked for that?'

We should now take up the question of what the maximum increase of (*rational*) requirements of evidence would be in order to justify (not verify) 'I know that *p*'. But since here and in the rest of the discussion I shall assume that there is a requirement of evidence for justifiably saying 'I know that *p*'—whatever the *p*—I should first of all offer some comments in support of this assumption.

In taking it for granted that if I say or think 'I know that *p*', I can *legitimately* ask at least myself what the evidence is, *irrespective of the kind of p*, but not irrespective of the situation, I am assuming something that can be termed propositional, as opposed to situational universality. Ayer, Austin, and others have argued against the propositional universality of the evidence requirement, that is, against the view that evidence can be properly asked for whatever the proposition claimed to be true. But, although I shall not further substantiate my disagreement here, I think they have only succeeded in showing that for some statements, for example, about my own pain, or where I live, a question of evidence is *in everyday life* out of place.[1] It is characteristic, however, that these cases are very near the limits of the useful application of 'I know'. Wittgenstein's remarks[2] are relevant here, undermining the distinctions between 'I know' and 'I do not know', and between 'I doubt that' and 'I do not doubt that', in reference to such statements as 'I am in pain'. And if it is ever pertinent to say *to somebody else* 'I *know* I am in pain', it seems to be in just those cases in which others might have reasons to doubt. In what follows I have for this reason not found it necessary to discuss occurrences of 'I know' where requirements of evidence are out of place.

Certain details in Ayer's exposition deserve closer attention here. In particular Ayer defends the view 'that there are some propositions that we can claim to know without having to know any other propositions as reasons for them'. 'If someone claimed to know that he was in pain or that he was daydreaming about being rich, it would seem absurd to ask him what evidence he had for believing that these things were so.'[3]

It would be absurd, perhaps, to expect A to put evidence at the disposal of B so that B could independently of A estimate the evidence A has at *his* disposal. For A to ask 'Am I really daydreaming about being rich?' is not absurd. He may have the suspicion that he is perhaps not day-dreaming but making pertinent reflections: 'What would I do if I doubled my income?' Or, he may on second thoughts find that he is or was dreaming about being a playboy—the question of money was not really touched on in the dream, he might have borrowed it. It is clear that as soon as one begins to become interested in exactly what happens and in classifying it by using certain terms, there are ample grounds for asking about evidence. If the evidence is expressed in words, propositions are formed, and while the dogmatist will claim them to be true, the sceptic will offer them for inspection.

In spite of his doubtful contention about the absurdity of asking (oneself) for evidence, the first quotation from Ayer, as far as I can see, expresses a tenable position. If I say 'I know that p',

---

[1] See, e.g., A. J. Ayer, 'Reply to Mr. Stigen', *Inquiry*, Vol. 4 (1961), No. 4, p. 292.
[2] *Philosophical Investigations* (Basil Blackwell, Oxford, 1958), § 246.
[3] 'Reply to Mr. Stigen', p. 292.

p may belong to a field in which I would not in everyday life form propositions in support of knowledge claims. The 'How do you know?' may be left unanswered, or one may say, 'Obviously I know', 'I know that I know', etc.

In certain dialogues, for example those concerning trustworthiness, or concerning introspective psychology, the status of knowledge which goes unchallenged in everyday life must be considered. The result seems always to be that in so far as the propositions state something at all, there are sources of error. Here the history of the psychology of degrees of intensity of attention affords an interesting field of study. This history shows that propositions which seemed to be based on the most direct, unquestionable introspection and which were made by trained observers, came eventually to be considered to be doubtful and not acceptable as expressions of knowledge.[1]

To return now to the question of what would be the maximum increase of (*rational*) requirements of evidence in order to justify the expression 'I know that *p*'. We can at least take it for granted at the outset that requirements may vary markedly, even in relation to a definite question, and that even in highly scientific contexts they can be very low.

Where would such a maximum increase land us? Would it *necessarily* prevent us from using the expression 'I know that *p*'? Would it at least as a matter of fact prevent us from using it? In order to answer this, some preliminaries will first have to be discussed.

First of all, let us examine the basis for contending that there are definite requirements to be satisfied in order justifiably to say 'I know'. Perhaps the best way of bringing out the fact that there are such requirements is to describe situations in which people are taken to task for having used the expression 'I know' (and similar phrases) when allegedly they were not entitled to do so. From a variety of cases—some of which might be constructed, but agreed upon by a panel of experts—one might then try to abstract rules. That is, one might try to construct more or less general requirement-hypotheses to fit the cases. (It would obviously be incautious to adopt general formulations proffered by people in concrete situations.) Such requirement formulations, with careful delimitation of intended range of validity, would not necessarily

[1] Cf. Charles Edward Spearman, *Psychology down the Ages* (Macmillan, London, 1937), Vol. I.

have any normative status *vis-à-vis* the language community, but they would at least represent attempts at clarifying and codifying the use of 'I know' in terms of definite requirements.

It should be remarked, however, that in no case should it be taken for granted that by increasing the number of cases surveyed more and more definite requirements fitting the cases could be constructed. In general there is in fact no good reason to believe in the 'existence' of use regularities susceptible to indefinite refinements in structure and content.

In what follows I shall speak *as if* one could abstract and extract requirements from surveying concrete cases of the use of 'I know'. It is at least a useful fiction for purposes of exposition.

4. MAXIMUM STRENGTHENING OF REQUIREMENTS IN THE FACE OF MISTAKES

Sometimes, even though the requirements of knowing have been satisfied, it is agreed a little later by those involved that after all there was a failure, a mistake.

The normal thing to do, if it is important not to fail, is to take heed of the mistakes, that is, to increase the requirements covering *that kind of situation* in which, admittedly, a mistake was made. Then next time in such a situation I shall not claim that I know; my claim will be more modest; or I shall apply some tests such that requirements of a higher level are satisfied: only then shall I say 'I know'.

Let us suppose that, unhappily, I make a mistake in the very same kind of situation in spite of applying the new, more severe tests. It will now be reasonable not only to increase requirements in the same kind of situation but also to increase them a little over a wider field. It is to some extent arbitrary how one is to assess the kind of situation at hand, and the consequences it has for other situations. A decision will be made, however, and it can be described as affecting not just the old kind of situation but also a more general kind.

If we suppose that this unhappy trend goes on for some time, there are two kinds of adjustments which are of special interest: one in which requirements are always given an increase of rigorousness and in an expanding area, without covering any one specified area, and one in which eventually the use of 'I know' is *in complete generality* taken to be incautious or inadvisable, other expressions being recommended in its place.

Let us inspect a hypothetical case study of how somebody might have come to 'know nothing':

'On certain occasions I discovered that a proposition of whose truth I had been sure, and on adequate evidence, was in fact false. Having had adequate grounds for my certainty, I may be said to have been justified in claiming to know, but in fact did not know. This discovery of error in respect of a previous well-supported certainty occurred on numerous new occasions, and each time I felt greater reluctance to claim to know. Eventually, I came to lose all confidence in claiming to know, since I was never sure the evidence excluded sources of error. Because of my never being sure, I cannot now be said to know anything.'

Now to what extent and in what way can such a report, biographical note, or psychological case study be relevant to the questions raised in the modern discussion on scepticism?

The actual use of 'I know' among psychiatrically normal persons of a language community is at least relevant to conclusions about how requirements remain constant through time intervals, or are increased or decreased in various kinds of situations. It is difficult to see how one could *legislate* about what would be a maximal increase beyond which one could not properly, or sincerely, refrain from using 'I know'. Therefore if such an unwillingness to use 'I know' became more and more widespread we might envisage circumstances in which *knowing* became not only unfashionable but totally extinct, in so far as 'I know' implies 'I am convinced'. Such a possibility is not to be excluded. After all, many other words have become employed more and more rarely and have tended to become extinct when occasions for their use grew sufficiently scarce, and there is no reason to think why this might not be so also in the case of 'I know'. As far as linguistic considerations are concerned, then, there are no objections to a process of development culminating in the extinction of the use of 'I know'.

But now let us look a little more closely at the repercussions of unexpected events upon standard requirements.

Repercussions upon standards may be said to have three dimensions: breadth, strength, and duration. Breadth measures the class of cases or situations covered. If I make a mistake in Latin grammar in spite of satisfying the standards, I may for a time increase my standards both in Latin and in other grammars, or only in Latin; or, where the failure is a damaging (shameful, embarrassing) one, I may for a short time show increased standards in every subject. (All within the very elastic limits of psychiatric normality.) This is the breadth dimension.

If we say that the increase may be very marked or only just perceptible, we are using the dimension of strength, which is self-explanatory.

Thirdly, if we receive no more rude shocks we simply change back to old habits and the increase in requirements gradually disappears. Here we have a time dimension, one that may be rationalized by dividing up time in terms of situations and by making use of inductive principles.

So much for the repercussions of failures. But successes and triumphs, that is, astonishing, unexpected, and important successes in 'I know' situations, also have repercussions. More often than not their effect may be a relaxing one: standards drop, and for this good, perhaps inductive, reasons can be given. As suggested by Ayer,[1] if an individual has a constant flow of successes, he may be led altogether to stop inquiring into evidence. This, however, would tend rather to mean that 'said by Mr. So-and-so' was to be taken as adequate evidence. On the other hand, successes can sometimes result in increases: for example, I may wish to retain a reputation that if *I* say I know, others may be perfectly sure that it is true.

So much for individual successes and vicissitudes. There are, of course, fluctuations in collectivities, too, in communities, inter-acting with individual experiences. During wars and other periods of intense community life and shared experiences the collective changes are more marked and more easily break through the individual variations. (One *should* know the enemy soldiers are cruel. Whatever the incidents which in other circumstances would certainly have repercussions, one must continue to be willing to say 'I know they are cruel'.) In some kinds of situation, require-ments for 'I know' can drop towards zero, in others they might increase towards infinity.

5. MAXIMUM AND ABNORMAL REPERCUSSIONS

Some changes in standards we are tempted to classify as 'irra-tional', others as 'rational'. Which classification we adopt depends to some extent upon our system of values. In any case there is

[1] *The Problem of Knowledge*, p. 33.

always the possibility of constructing a set of rules from which what *we* consider rational changes of standards can be derived.

Suppose in giving a lesson in geometry I say that I know π to be 3·14158 . . . and later admit failure, being convinced by others that π is 3·14159 . . . According to my (and many others') criteria, I would behave irrationally if this prevented me from answering positively to the question whether I know that 5 multiplied by 6 is 30. It would be much too drastic a personal reaction to my failure for it to form the basis of a mistrust in my 'knowledge' of the simple multiplication table; such a repercussion upon standards would be unreasonable. But sometimes severe repercussions *are* reasonable. And even where they are not, the question of the use of 'I know' cannot be solved by legislation according to the way rationalists would wish it to be used.

A succession of failures may cause me to refrain from using 'I know' either in important matters or generally. The two cases are not as different as might be thought at first glance. If I renounce its use in important matters I may still use it loosely.[1] ('My wife never lets me out, you know.'—'*I* know?'—'Of course, I'm telling you.') If reproved for doing this ('But you have just demonstratively refused to say *you* know what would be the right thing to do in our present predicament!'), I may point to the difference. ('Of course, you and I don't strictly speaking know this about my wife. Have you lost your sense of proportion?') When one is in a bad predicament and conscious of one's responsibility, one finds it irresponsible to say 'I know'. Thus, to refrain from using 'I know' in important matters is in certain senses to give it up in general, as far as cognitive, serious purposes are concerned.

And still within the psychiatrically normal—I may refrain from using it in important matters for the rest of my life—especially if I died very soon. Or I may promise myself to refrain from it, but fail, an unwillingness to say 'I know' might, after all, in some situations in some communities be as embarrassing as refraining from saying 'thank you'.

To refrain from using 'I know' in important matters may also express one's awareness of a *general fallibility*. According to Austin,

---

[1] This sounds as if I were to say to myself 'From now on, do not use "I know" in important matters'. The adjustments, modifications in usage, are, of course, normally made without articulation. Freud would call them 'prebewusst' (preconscious); there are no barriers to their being made conscious (as with the unconscious), they simply do not occur to one.

however, general fallibility by itself cannot rationally be a motive for saying 'I know nothing' (in the modern sceptic's way); there must be additional premises. If stakes are small and there are discoverable differences in the chances of a mistake, why should I *always* avoid claiming to know?

Yet, and perhaps in extension of Austin's point, in matters of life and death, the awareness of the importance, the awareness of the terrible consequences of failure, may rationally motivate me to renounce the use of 'I know', whatever the evidence. In relation to certain subgroups of situations, therefore, 'I *know* nothing' may be an adequate expression of my opinion and attitudes.[1] As pointed out by Ayer and others, in saying I know something, I am vouching for it; thus my saying it has some important social implications. But then if I find it unjustifiable to vouch for (and, perhaps, to swear to) something, finding that to do so would be inconsistent with my value system, I may stick to my *personal* conviction, yet still in a rational way, and in view of conceived failures *abstain* from using 'I know', or even find it justifiable to say 'I know nothing'.

Socially I perform my duty as a witness, for example, when I painstakingly describe the evidence I think I have, adding on request any further information about my personal conviction or belief, and my personal estimate of the chances of my being mistaken. The rest I leave to the jury and others concerned. If some will say that in the light of my total statement I know, or that I do not know, I will not object. *They* may say that I know even if I would not. Only if I were forced to take a stand would I give my reasons for avoiding the use of the distinction between known and not known in questions of life and death. If, on the other hand, I do employ the distinction and am sure about something, so long as certain other requirements are satisfied I would be perfectly

[1] J. L. Austin, 'Other Minds', *Philosophical Papers* (Clarendon Press, Oxford, 1961), pp. 65–7. It is not entirely clear to me why general fallibility in the sense of 'acute sense of general fallibility' should not rationally ('psychiatrically rationally') prevent somebody using 'I know' or adequately expressing his attitude by 'I know nothing'. It all depends on the way of announcing 'Alas! we are all of us always fallible' and 'I know nothing'. If the announcement amounts to a knowledge claim, a position Sextus calls 'Academic' (cf. Chap. 1, pp. 4 and 12, above) is taken. There are some very strong objections, some of them formulated by Sextus himself, to that position. If something less than a knowledge claim is made, and the way of announcement is one of those Sextus refers to as his 'sceptical phrases', I see no reason to reject 'I know nothing'. According to some definitions of philosophy, it would not belong to philosophy, but that should not detract from the propriety of the expression.

right to *say* 'I know that so-and-so'. And this would continue to be so even if subsequent events proved me wrong. For then what was wrong was what I said was the case, not my saying that it was the case. It would be misleading here, too, to say that I did not know that *not* so-and-so if the context suggests that this implies some degree of blame: 'You should have known that not so-and-so, but you didn't.' The circumstances in which it is right to *say* 'I know that so-and-so', even if what I claim is subsequently shown to be false, are precisely those in which it would be wrong for me to say 'I know that not so-and-so', despite the fact that this latter claim would have been true.

The most important point for us here is to make a distinction between having a piece of knowledge and having good, standard, or adequate reason, evidence, or grounds for being certain. If I hesitate in, or abstain from, saying 'I know it' because I see (am sure I see) a *remote possibility* of being wrong, this does not necessarily violate any explicit or implicit rules of ordinary language. It may be a symptom of overcautiousness, hypochondria, hyperactivity of the imagination, or inability to square up to some formidable responsibility, but all of this may still be within the range of psychiatric normality. My mind is not deranged, I am still a member of my language community.

Moreover I may be perfectly aware that others are much more free than I am in their use of 'I know', and disapprove of this— all *within* the framework of our common language which is not after all the monopoly of but one type of person.

One might bring out the cognitive factor in abstinence from the use of 'I know', its rationality, in terms of inductions and of consideration of limitations of terminologies in terms of fruitfulness. If there have been more failures than were expected and are tolerated within a sphere of action or investigation, it is reasonable to increase standards in order to decrease the risk of a continuing high rate of failure. No doubt some kind of inductive conceptual framework is best suited to articulate the rationality of the increase. Secondly, the fruitfulness of a distinction has its limitations. Sometimes the social aspect of vouching and guaranteeing is considered unnecessary. Why then use 'I know'? If what I aim at is an independent evaluation of *p* by others, I modify your wording as a rational means for reaching that end. (*A*: But do you *know*? *B*: I am convinced, but *this time* you'd better see for yourself.)

6. 'I KNOW NOTHING'—GENERAL LINGUISTIC COUNTERARGUMENT

There have been various arguments designed to rebut the claim that one can reasonably abstain from the use of 'I know', or the slightly different and stronger claim that the utterance 'I know nothing' can be in order.

An argument that we certainly know at least one thing is sometimes based on a kind of linguistic *a priori*: since there is 'in our language' (I should prefer 'in the vocabulary of our language') a distinction between 'knowing' and 'not-knowing', there *must* be an exemplified difference between what is known and what is not known. How else could the distinction have been introduced and understood? After all, we *learn* a difference between the terms from actual instances; so if there *are* no instances we cannot learn it. In much the same vein it has been argued that not all things can be illusory, at least some things must be veridical. Unless this were so the notion of illusoriness would lose all its point.

But surely a child could be taught to use 'illusory' perfectly correctly by instances such as the difference between the neighbours' spurious Santa Claus (being only the father in disguise) and its own family's real Santa Claus, between the neighbours' naughty boy's spurious courage and his father's genuine courage? In a similar way generation *n* of adults introduces the difference in terms of their (non-illusory) ideals and the (illusory) ones of generation *n* − 1. The difference between 'illusory' and 'not illusory', as well as those between 'known' and 'not known', 'veridical' and 'not veridical', can be introduced and learned on the basis of the beliefs or convictions of the persons concerned. Whether the beliefs are correct or not (in an absolute sense) makes no difference whatsoever.[1]

If a boy *A* has learned to use 'illusory' and 'not illusory' simply by 100 examples, and later in life he considers the cases of non-illusory things to be similar to the cases of the illusory, we may find him saying *all* things are illusory.

There is nevertheless a way in which a paradigmatic learning theory may be important in understanding rather different positions that have been called sceptical. Thus, when writing his famous 'Why Nothing Can Be Known' (*Quod nihil scitur*), Sanches

---

[1] One can learn by denotation or by connotation. 'Perpetuum mobile', 'eternal bliss', and many other expressions are learned by their connotations.

cannot properly be said to have overlooked that he knew he had (or did not have) toothache. There are several uses of 'I know that *p*' (and related terms) and one of them relates to 'matters important to the soul', such as religious, metaphysical, and scientific doctrines. This kind of use was already well established by the time of Sextus Empiricus, and Sanches too had learned it. Moreover, he may be said to have learned it paradigmatically, seeing it applied solely in connection with *doctrines*, and not in connection with utterances such as 'I have toothache'. But then by applying the known *vs.* not known distinction within the sphere of that particular use, Sanches neither had nor did not have toothache, in so far as neither the assertion that one has nor the assertion that one does not have toothache constitutes a doctrine.

The point of this example is that the terms 'sceptic', 'sceptical', and 'scepticism' have been applied for a very long time, and they are closely connected with uses of 'knowing' which may well not be the *first* uses one learns as a child, but uses which one in any case learns somehow, and in very much the same way as the first uses. A debate on scepticism might certainly refer only to 'knowing' on the infantile level, but it ought to be clear that this does not cover all interesting uses of 'knowing' and especially not those important in philosophical literature.

7. CIRCULARITY OF THE SCEPTIC'S ARGUMENT

There is another short-cut aimed at avoiding scepticism: it is claimed that the utterance 'I do not know anything' is absurd or inconsistent because I implicitly assert that I *know* that I do not know anything. But this antisceptical argument is untenable. It rests on the false assumption that the ways of announcing 'I do not know anything' can be reduced to one, namely, 'I know that', or to some others from which 'I know that' can be derived. There are, however, a number of ways of announcing which do not fulfil this requirement, for example, 'I am perfectly convinced that', 'I believe that'. Sextus Empiricus can be studied with profit on this point.

Let us now turn to the utterance which we are presuming to be made in complete seriousness, 'I cannot get to know anything'. Against its tenability, considered as a statement, there are strong arguments of various kinds. Let us first consider those arguments that claim the existence of conclusive, unretractable, irrevocable evidence.

8. THE CONCLUSIVENESS OF CONCLUSIVE EVIDENCE —SOCIAL AND LINGUISTIC RIGHTNESS AND TRUTH

In philosophical debate there are still symptoms of a confusion between the right to say something, e.g. the right to say 'It is true that p', 'There can be no doubt that p', 'Of course, p', 'In this I cannot possibly be mistaken', and the certainty that p is true. If 'I know that p' is interpreted in this confused way, the statement may be thought to be unretractable if in fact I had the right to say it, and whether or not p is later considered false. Let the relevant distinctions be repeated once more.

To assert 'I have conclusive (unretractable, irrevocable, decisive) evidence', or 'This closes the matter once and for all', or 'Here no doubt is possible', or 'It cannot conceivably be otherwise', or 'This is absolutely certain', is justified in everyday life if certain requirements are fulfilled. In the course of a dialogue standards may vary, just as in the case of 'I know'. Unexpected kinds of failures and successes can occur, and they have repercussions of various kinds. Here is a little dialogue for illustration:

A: The two papers *are* in this room.
B: That is simply inconceivable, I have searched for them all day in this very room. It is absolutely impossible that they are here. I know they are not here. The evidence is utterly conclusive.
A: Well, look here then. Here is one of them.
B: So it is. I don't understand this.
A: Should we look for the other?
B: Well, yes, we'd better do that.
A: It is not inconceivable that the other is here?
B: Hm.

If B had searched the room all day, one would allow that he was entitled to use expressions like 'absolutely impossible', 'perfectly certain', 'utterly conclusive'. However, there is not the slightest guarantee that he would not have to retract. The justifiability of *exclaiming* 'conclusive!' does not exclude having made a mistake.

Douglas Arner stresses that in the face of conclusive evidence, any further demand for evidence is unintelligible:

'It is quite true that grounds treated as conclusive are always short of a demonstration and even occasionally prove inadequate. The important thing is that conclusive evidence *concludes*: no demand for more evidence in the face of conclusive evidence is intelligible.'[1]

If Arner could only tell us what conclusive evidence looks like so that we could infallibly recognize it and avoid talking unintelligibly! But his attention soon shifts to what *counts* as conclusive:

'What counts as conclusive evidence is a matter of tacit, continuing agreement among the users of the language. We learn early that we are not to claim knowledge unless we have met certain requirements in the way of qualifications and evidence. These requirements are founded chiefly on what grounds have proved adequate almost all of the time . . .'

Here there seems to be no distinction made between 'The evidence for p is conclusive' and 'The evidence for p satisfies what counts for conclusive evidence'.[2] The latter may be true despite the falsity of the former, that is, if 'conclusive evidence' is taken to imply truth, and I think it does for most interpretations. 'I have conclusive evidence for p, but p may be false' does not work.

On the most primitive everyday level there is, maybe, a good deal of tacit agreement about what counts as conclusive evidence, but it certainly seems more appropriate to reserve the conceptual distinction between conclusive and non-conclusive evidence for where there are explicit premises and conclusions. The distinction seems to belong to that level of talk. And at that level one is aware of the difference between the justifiable *calling* of some evidence 'conclusive' and conclusive evidence itself. Here as with knowing, I may be perfectly right in saying something but completely wrong in what I say. What counts as conclusive evidence that a person is dead is, for obvious reasons, rather strong evidence among responsible physicians, but once in a million or more cases a frightful mistake is discovered. Some people, of course, will find

[1] Douglas Arner, 'On Knowing', *Philosophical Review*, Vol. LXVIII (1959), p. 88.
[2] The same lack of clear distinction between social and cognitive factors goes back to the father of British common-sense philosophy, Thomas Reid, who insists that if anything is self-evident, then 'to desire more evidence is absurd' (*Essays on the Intellectual Powers of Man*, ed. A. D. Woozley (London, 1941), pp. vii, viii), and that this is a valid argument against sceptics. It is perhaps absurd to say 'This is self-evident, let me look for more evidence', but not 'this fulfils standard requirements justifying the pronouncement "this is self-evident", but let us look for some more evidence than the required'.

these cases uninteresting because for all practical, normal, ordinary, everyday purposes they just do not occur, but others will find them extremely interesting. 'This evidence is (already) conclusive. May I, please, have some more?' This would be a rather original demand, but at least to me perfectly intelligible. For there may be people who make the mistake of not taking the evidence to be conclusive, and they may want me to be able to add some pieces, some additional witnesses, etc. 'This evidence must count as (can safely be treated as) conclusive. But may I, please, have some more?' This kind of question is not only intelligible, but to pose it may sometimes be a duty. There are no definite requirements of conclusiveness, they vary in relation to a number of factors. (Responsibilities, consequences of failure, past experience within a narrow field to which p belongs, past experience in a broader field, etc.)

The inadequacy of the everyday and the normality arguments for establishing what is conclusive evidence is well illustrated if one considers utterances such as 'We are never justified in being absolutely certain', or 'I do not know anything whatsoever', or 'Nothing *can* be known'. We just have to reflect that there are, on the one hand, requirements for being justified in *saying* such things (try it out at some evening parties!), and, on the other, *admitted* failures; that is, those engaged may, after some time, retract and say 'I *do* know something, after all'. Nor is the requirement for announcing 'failure' universally higher than that for announcing 'success'; that is, it is always equally possible that some failures may turn into successes.

I think we can safely say that sceptical locutions in everyday life are not intended to cover, systematically and in relation to current conceptual frameworks, an assertion 'I do not know anything'. Compared with their epistemologically intended counterparts, such everyday locutions are offhand and unsystematic verbal gestures. And even if they are subjected to some form of regulation in the shape of justifiability requirements, these latter are of a fairly indeterminate and unconceptualized sort.

Instead of everyday utterances, therefore, we shall take up sentences such as 'I do not know anything' as they appear to be placed in philosophical debates, in a wide sense of 'debate'; that is, in discussions that intend such sentences in a more systematic and conceptualized way than that in which they are used in everyday life.

9. EXAMPLES OF THERE BEING SOMETHING WE KNOW OR CAN KNOW

Recently epistemologists have provided us with many good examples of the kinds of things we know or can know. The method by which they are introduced goes more or less as follows. First, a certain situation is described and then in that situation we are to suppose an utterance of the expression 'I know' (or something equivalent). Then the author of the example, sometimes after adding in some convincing details, appeals to the reader, as much as to say 'Now you see, you doubting Thomases! Repent!' But of course, if the examples are to have their proper force in a debate, the adversary must not be thus pushed or terrorized into accepting them. One particular method of persuasion, astonishingly common all the way from Plato to Austin, amounts to little more than saying something like 'Suppose I see an elephant and I say "I see an elephant", could I be wrong? Would I ever have to retract?'

The procedure is intended to convince us that there are frequent and indisputable cases of our knowing that things are what they are, or as they are. Austin, for example, asserts that some statements 'are *in fact* incorrigible'. They are 'quite certainly, definitely, and unretractably *true*'.[1] And, implicitly, he takes this to amount to a proof that there are *p*'s such that I know that *p*.

Thus, 'if I watch for some time an animal a few feet in front of me, in a good light, if I prod it perhaps, sniff, and take note of the noises it makes, I may say "That's a pig" '. This statement 'will be "incorrigible", nothing could be produced that would show that I had made a mistake'.[2] Here Austin will have us assume, entirely on his own authority, that he *is* watching for some time, that it *is* an animal he is watching, that the light *is* good enough for the purposes at hand, and that he *is* sniffing the animal in question. By being made to postulate the truth of so many premises we become confused as to how the conclusion could possibly be false. But of course we should recall that an implication comprising a conjunction of a swarm of antecedents and only one consequent is among the very weakest that can be made.

It may be conceded that Austin, under most circumstances in which this could have happened, would be perfectly *justified* in

[1] J. L. Austin, *Sense and Sensibilia*, p. 115 (Austin's italics).
[2] *Ibid.*, p. 114.

saying what in the example he is supposed to have said. But it is hard to accept that 'nothing could be produced that would show that I had made a mistake'. Very much depends on one's acquaintances, whether they have a penchant towards practical jokes or include an amateur magician. (If we are asked about pigs with a professional magician near by, we are wise to bet only a small amount and keep our 'knowing' under strict control.) In short, even a good amateur magician could bring us into a situation such as the one Austin describes and provoke us into saying 'I know this is a pig', and soon after make us *retract*.

There is something to be said in general about examples which contain plenty of detail about what has already been done in order to ensure that *p* actually *is* the case. The doubter or disbeliever is, as it were, politely but authoritatively requested to accept all the details as true of the situation in which 'I know that *p*' was uttered. He has then nothing to complain about. But it is easy to forget that if the example were true to life, the doubter should have had the opportunity to inspect the details for himself; he would not have to rely on hearsay.

Consider in this respect the many reports of ghosts, for example, which *if* the apparently true details concerning the situations are accepted, are overwhelmingly convincing. The contemporary ghost-hunter, however, has professional rules which make him for the most part withhold judgment until he has the opportunity to report about the situation himself.

Consider another example: someone remarks in casual conversation 'As a matter of fact I live in Oxford'. According to Austin,[1] the speaker 'knows it to be true (or, if he is lying, false)'. But many people are in trouble because they *want* to be able to say truthfully 'I live in the town (city) so-and-so'—because an authority of some sort can otherwise deprive them of certain privileges—but they are uncertain. The criteria are complicated and their satisfaction not always clear. Incidentally a famous, rather unruly and restless 'sceptic' in the history of modern philosophy, and author of 'Of the Uncertainty and Vanity of the Arts and Sciences' (*De incertitudine et vanitate de scientiarum et artium*), Agrippa of Nettesheim, could probably only rarely give an account of where he lived, if he could have been said to live in any definite place at all. Recently J. Wasiutyński[2] has assured us, however, that

---

[1] *Ibid.*, pp. 117–18.
[2] *Universet* (Oslo: Universitetsforlaget, 1963), p. 130.

there 'can no longer be any doubt that we live in a spiral nebula'. So, is nobody to worry any more about where he lives?

The gist of the matter seems to be this: We take 'I live in Oxford' to be beyond any doubt and requiring no evidence, because we place ourselves in a *particular situation* in which we have no *reason* or *incentive* to doubt. But the claim that I live in Oxford is not made more certain by being expressed in a situation in which the reasons and incentives to doubt its truth are reduced. To say that it was would be to misunderstand the relation between a statement and the conditions in which it is made. The conditions are not to be seen as part of the claim, and therefore cannot be taken to determine whether or not it has the property of 'being certain'. A claim made in one situation which excludes reasons and incentives to doubt its truth can be made in different conditions where such reasons and incentives once more come into play.

Consider how in casual conversation the requirement of evidence for 'I know that *p*' may be so small as to make the claim to know wellnigh gratuitous, whereas in criminal cases, for example, the requirement for evidence must be adduced. The difference here is largely one in the requirements of justification, and as such strictly related to questions of responsibility which may be near zero in casual conversation and 'infinite' for an eyewitness in a murder case.

A final example:

> 'If I carefully scrutinize some patch of colour in my visual field, take careful note of it, know English well, and pay scrupulous attention to just what I'm saying, I may say "It seems to me now as if I were seeing something pink"; and nothing whatever could be produced as showing that I had made a mistake.'[1]

That Austin, after all that care and effort, and no doubt at all paying close attention to exactly what he is saying, still uses the term 'seems' suggests immediately something rather suspicious here, as does also the use of 'as if I were'. There is, in short, ample indication that something could well happen to make us assume he had made a mistake. Or so Austin's words suggest. If, on the other hand, the situation (as he judged it) warranted perfect certainty, then what he in fact uttered is grossly misleading. Surely it would have been more correct for him to avoid the hedging forms of expression and say 'I am seeing something pink'.

[1] *Sense and Sensibilia*, p. 114.

I shall not try to introduce anything new into the difficult contemporary discussion on certainty and knowledge within the field of immediate perception. Austin has himself suggested many sources of error and therefore of possible retractions.

The crux of the matter can be put in this way: a proof or strong argument in favour of incorrigi*bility*, unretracta*bility*, and related *-bilities* must be more than an inductively based prediction. It should somehow derive from contemplation both of the nature of the incorrigible statement and of the subject covered by such a statement. Just this, however, is very hard to achieve. In fact Austin himself points out how difficult it is to delimit certain *kinds* of statements as incorrigible by virtue of their subject-matter (e.g. sense-data) or other characteristics.

It seems, therefore, that incorrigibility claims are essentially based on convictions that in the particular case there could not be any source of error, both in the usual sense of 'source of error *worth mentioning*' and in the sense of no source of error even of the more remote kinds that we neglect in daily life. This conviction is based on a trust that one's imagination works as it should at the time of making up one's mind about the corrigibility, when one is 'looking' for sources of error. So incorrigibility theses are testable by future events; they are vulnerable. Simply to add to one's statement 'And what I have just said is incorrigible' does not close the matter.

Let us look at the discussion on incorrigibility dialectically. Strings of striking cognitive successes of incorrigibility claims may justifiably influence the standards for incorrigibility or un-retractability claims, making them less rigorous. On the other hand, series of striking cognitive malfunctions may justifiably influence standards by making them appreciably rigorous. What is remarkable here is the 'feedback mechanism', the inherent norms, mores, or institutions effecting changes in certain directions.

Just how far can the changes of standard bring us? In fact, there seem to be no limits; they can be lowered or increased indefinitely in the sense that having reached a certain height or depth, there will always be the possibility of an additional increase or decrease.

A criticism of contemporary debate on (epistemological) scepticism is that it does not seem to take into account the dynamics of standard fluctuations. But fluctuations affect the application of all so-called closure-expressions, such as 'conclusive evidence', 'incorrigible statement', 'indubitable utterance', and 'definite establishment of truth'.

If the fluctuations are taken to result from the operation of some kind of factors, if, in terms of methodology, they are taken to be the dependent variable, what are the independent variables? One might be inclined to say that it is our experience that affects the standards and determines the fluctuations. This suggests a kind of empiricism à la J. S. Mill in which whatever affects us, hence also our raising and lowering of standards, is something in our experience. However, such a way of putting it would be misleading because we are ourselves in some sense interposed between the happenings and the 'resulting' fluctuations. There is a factor of making, supporting, applying rules or mores which cannot be accounted for as long as we use a model of causation, of happenings, *causing* fluctuations.

However, it is not our aim here to find out why or even how fluctuations operate. It suffices to notice that if the dynamics of fluctuations are not explicitly taken into account, one and the same statement may justifiably occasion opposite estimations as regards incorrigibility, unretractability, unquestionableness, etc. The situation in which the statement is supposed to occur is, in such cases, placed as a member of different series of situations. If it is taken as following upon a long series of cognitive failures, a verdict of 'corrigible' may be adequate, but if it is taken as following an opposite series the adequate verdict could be 'incorrigible'. As long as they are not explicitly related to the series the verdicts are mutually inconsistent. But, of course, once that is done they are compatible.

Recent discussions concerning examples of conclusive evidence and incorrigible statements support the simple prediction that the participants aiming at undermining the examples will always find (practical, particular) sources of error (if the examples are not circular), and that the participants aiming at saving at least one example will be able to introduce modifications so as to eliminate those (particular, practical) sources. In fact, Sextus Empiricus's maxim 'not more than' seems eminently suited to the debate: the arguments for incorrigibility are not decisively stronger than the arguments against. A general conclusion unrelated to the dynamics of standard fluctuations, to the effect that there *are* cases of conclusive evidence, seems equally unconvincing as one to the effect that there are not.

10. EXAMPLES OF EVIDENCE FUSING WITH THE EVIDENCED

'Why on earth should one think that such verification can't ever be conclusive?' It is Austin asking the question and his theme is statements *in need of* verification.[1]

'If, for instance, you tell me there's a telephone in the next room, and (feeling mistrustful) I decide to verify this . . . I can take it to pieces a bit and find out, or actually use it for ringing somebody up—and perhaps get them to ring me up too, just to make sure.'

The object has then 'stood up to amply enough tests to establish that it really is a telephone; and it isn't just that, for everyday or practical or ordinary purposes, enough is *as good as* a telephone; what meets all these tests just *is* a telephone, no doubt about it'.[2]

Or, to extract the principle, something's membership of a class of things is *for all practical purposes* conclusively established if results are positive when the thing is subjected to a finite battery of tests.

But, alas, do we, when trying to verify concrete examples, test the identity of a thing as to what it is for everyday, practical, or ordinary purposes? If we sometimes have other (legitimate or illegitimate) purposes, and the thing then has to be classed differently, it may turn out that those other non-practical or unordinary or uneveryday purposes are relevant.

Let us nevertheless leave that point and consider whether 'a case can be closed' after a finite series of tests have been performed. In the case of the telephone, I have no concrete objection: positive results from the four tests would be, I am perfectly convinced, enough for me to exclaim 'Then this *is* a telephone!', because nothing but telephones, and only telephones, satisfy the four tests, as far as I can see.

But what if the question of a telephone in the next room emerged during a police search? We are still only interested in situations in which maximum requirements are made. David Krueger, one of the greatest impostors of all time, and many

---

[1] *Sense and Sensibilia*, p. 118. Of course, in what I have been saying in the foregoing there is no doubting about the *justification* of saying 'I verified it' in very many situations. What has been discussed among verification specialists is verifiability in highly technical (in part purely logical) senses under maximum-requirement conditions.

[2] *Ibid.*, p. 119.

lesser crooks, have had telephones ('real' ones?) installed which buzz at convenient intervals during crucial conferences. The voices of very important people are heard over the phone, and some impressive business is cleared up; the voices, however, are from a gramophone or tape recorder. In the spying profession innocent instruments such as telephones are completely rebuilt in order to furnish less innocent instruments. They still at least look like telephones. The instruments must perhaps satisfy all Austin's four telephone requirements, or, more correctly, must be such that a suspicious person will normally come to that conclusion after a thorough search. In short, the four requirements (in part seemingly, in part really) being satisfied, the thing may still be a lot of things other than or besides a telephone.

But enough of this! The real point of the example is to show that the idea of a finite battery of tests for identification purposes brings in no radically new factors. Especially when the tests have to be performed one at a time, as is the case in the telephone story, it is always possible for new sources of error to develop with time.

Thus our ultimate view will be unaffected by this story, nor do we believe that the discussion over (concrete) examples is likely to come to an end.

II. INCORRIGIBILITY AND FALLIBILITY

An essential characteristic of human fallibility is the unpredict-ableness of what kind of mistake will be the next. If it were true that human fallibility had (*a*) infallibly ascertainable limits which (*b*) were infallibly identifiable in certain particular cases, there would be human fallibility in one sphere and human infallibility in another.[1] But the awkwardness of the human predicament is due precisely to the unpredictable failures. However long the series of successes and however well the field of these successes can be delimited, this trait of general human fallibility does not change.

Let us for a moment grant that such is our human situation and consider some of the consequences.

Does this situation make it universally justifiable, and in fact

---

[1] One is reminded of the possibility of constructing infallible statements ('This is pink') and fallible ones ('This is magenta'), or infallible ('This seems to me pink') and fallible ones ('This is pink'). Do we really mean to say that here is an infallible difference?

true, to add that 'I may be wrong'? If so, it will always be justified and true, where I have already said 'I know that p', to add
'but I may be wrong'. But this disqualifies my utterance 'I know
that p', and the only thing to do will be to give up ever using 'I
know' and to answer, being prodded, 'I do not *know* whether p
is true or false' and 'I do not know and cannot know anything'.

Here, then, is a possibility of deriving modern scepticism from
a doctrine of general fallibility.

But there is weakness both in that doctrine and in the derivation of scepticism from it. If we ask 'Is the doctrine of general
fallibility intended to apply to itself?', a positive answer at least
opens the door to allegations that human beings might, after all,
be pretty infallible, which again makes the doctrine useless for
deriving 'but I may be wrong' as a *general* addition to 'I know that
p'. A negative answer, on the other hand, provides us with an
instance of a statement that is incorrigible and true; in that case
'I may be wrong' is false if this statement is inserted for 'p'. The
derivation, therefore, collapses, at least in its completely general
form.

More important are the considerations adduced by Austin.[1]
Human fallibility involves fallibility in keeping promises and in
many other important social transactions. Why does this not prevent us, and why *should* it not prevent us, from promising?
Austin stresses that there must be special reasons in the given case
for suspecting a break of promise in order to make it rational to
avoid promising (because of fallibility). Similarly with knowing:
only where there is something special that points to an important
source of error should fallibility prevent me from using 'I know'.
General fallibility may be generally admitted, but not fallibility in
any definite concrete case. That is, general fallibility is not per-
mitted to constitute a justification for comprehensively avoiding
'I know'.

---

[1] Austin ('Other Minds', p. 66) says that 'being aware that you may be mistaken
doesn't mean merely being aware that you are a fallible human being: it means that
you have some concrete reason to suppose that you may be mistaken in this case.
Just as "but I may fail" does not mean merely "but I am a weak human being" (in
which case it would be no more exciting than adding "D.V."): it means that there
is some concrete reason for me to suppose that I shall break my word. It is naturally
always possible ("humanly" possible) that I may be mistaken or may break my word,
but that by itself is no bar against using the expressions "I know" and "I promise"
as we do in fact use them.' Very well, but from *using* 'I know' in a socially convenient
way it does not follow that anything is known. Cf. our use of 'demon', 'devil',
'superhuman', 'eternal fame', 'never to be forgotten', etc.

(*A*: Tell the judge *you* know that it was he who did it. *B*: What a responsibility to take! And do I really know? I am but a fallible human being. *A*: That holds for all of us. Go on, tell him, you coward.)[1]

In all concrete cases in which it involves a social responsibility to say 'I know', general fallibility cannot be invoked. The same holds good for all cases in which the sentence 'I do *not* know' is conceptualized[2] within a framework such that it implies awareness of how to know that one does not know, awareness of how to get adequate evidence, and of what kind of evidence is lacking. Here too general fallibility cannot count as an adequate argument in favour of the exclusion of knowledge.

Nevertheless a dialogue starting in the midst of everyday concerns, may reach stages at which general fallibility becomes relevant in the argument. This we will discuss later.

12. CORRIGIBILITY AS A REQUIREMENT OF SCIENTIFIC KNOWLEDGE

Although a justified utterance 'I know that *p*' is not incompatible with the general possibility of error, it is, as we noted, inconsistent with a concomitantly uttered 'I may be wrong'. What then is the core of a reasonable and workable incorrigibility requirement of knowledge? It can be stated in very few words:[3]

One cannot say 'I know it, but I may be wrong', 'I know that *p*, but there is a chance that *p* is false', 'I know that *p*, but some time ago I knew that not-*p*', 'I know that *p*, but next year maybe I'll

---

[1] Suppose N.N. says 'Alas, I am always liable to be mistaken in whatever I say, but I *know* London is sometimes rather foggy', would we not interpret this 'but' to refer to an exception from the liability? That is, in his use of the term 'know', N.N. excludes the possibility of being mistaken.

[2] It seems that Wittgenstein would deny the necessity of a conceptual framework here and hold that all 'proper' use of the expression 'not know' implies awareness of how to know.

[3] Ayer puts it elegantly:'—it is inconsistent to say "I know but I may be wrong". But the reason why this is inconsistent is that saying "I know" offers a guarantee which saying "I may be wrong" withdraws' (*The Problem of Knowledge*, p. 25). It is inconsistent, in a social sense, to *give* a guarantee and immediately *withdraw* it. Making a gift and withdrawing it are two actions related to each other in a particular way. But *what* is guaranteed in asserting 'I know that *p*'? That it is so, that *p* is true. The wrongness referred to in the qualification 'but I may be wrong' is then wrongness about *p*'s being true, that is, the falseness of *p*—that it is *not* as I say it is. This is the crux of the matter, not the inconsistency of two behaviours as such. However important it is not to neglect the performative aspect of 'I know', it is the cognitive inconsistency that counts in the debate on scepticism.

know that not-*p*'. That is, if I have said 'I know that *p*', and later I am convinced of not-*p*, or feel uncertain about *p*'s truth, I shall have to retract: I shall have to admit 'I *do not* and *did not ever* know *p*'.

The nature of the requirement of incorrigibility can be further clarified by discussing its relation to statements made about scientific knowledge. This knowledge is said to be essentially corrigible, liable to revision, approximate, never absolutely certain, more or less uncertain, never more than probable, the best we have but imperfect, always containing errors, often partially or totally modified, sometimes swept away during scientific revolutions. Often these things are also predicated of 'human knowledge' in general. But what then of our incorrigibility requirement?

Let us first notice that these characterizations nearly always refer to scientific knowledge *in general* or large bodies of doctrines, theories, hypotheses, and so on, taken together. Very rarely do they refer to single statements, or to single definite occurrences of 'I know' (etc.) uttered by a scientist.

If we glance at histories of science, or at historical accounts of theories, such as atomic views about matter, we find ample reference to the knowledge of the times—including doctrines which have subsequently been revised or completely abandoned. But we discover no (or practically no) kind of statements inconsistent with the 'prohibited' locutions listed at the head of this section or, rather, with their equivalent third-person locutions. For instance, we do not find 'Descartes knew that *p*, but already Newton knew that not-*p*', 'He knew *p*, whereas we now know not-*p*', etc.

We do find, on the other hand, that certain knowledge was corrected, improved upon, and so on, but still 'in the abstract', the term *knowledge* being used, not the verb, and with no recourse to particular statements.

There is thus no direct contradiction between the corrigibility view of knowledge especially common in reference to science, and the incorrigibility requirement for 'I know that *p*'. Perhaps, in view of the tendency to use the noun 'knowledge' in the former case and the verb 'know' in the latter, it might be wise to talk about the 'incorrigibility requirement of *knowing*', and the 'corrigible and fallible nature of scientific *knowledge*'.

Only persons can know. Yet concepts of knowledge can be,

and have been, construed in such a way that knowledge is impersonal. Knowledge can be stored away in libraries, whereas knowing cannot. If knowledge can be transferred to books and put on tape, the existence of knowing readers and listeners can, of course, no longer be guaranteed by the existence of knowledge. Thus, the distinction between knowing and knowledge can be of *some* help in avoiding certain pitfalls when contemplating fallibility and incorrigibility. The distinction is, however, not clear enough or simple enough in actual use to be of decisive value. If I say 'I know that *p*' it is perfectly proper and legitimate to take this to imply that I have a piece of knowledge, namely that *p*. But this piece of knowledge must be true, that is, partake of the incorrigibility of truth. Again, if I tend to use 'I know' repeatedly during conferences or lectures, or refer to large groups of statements saying 'All this I know', there will be whole bodies of claimed knowledge for which the incorrigibility requirement is normally claimed to be satisfied. Thus knowledge claims may sometimes imply an incorrigibility claim even when they refer to a whole body of doctrines or statements. Appeal to usage, then, has only limited value.

Perhaps some of the uneasiness we sometimes experience when advocating the incorrigibility requirement for 'I know' stems from a faint association with a preposterous infallibility claim for scientific (or other) knowledge: the claim that the body of science, an encyclopedia of scientific knowledge, is such that no error can or will be found and corrected.

13. CAN THE INCORRIGIBILITY REQUIREMENT EVER BE SATISFIED?

Accepting the idea that knowing involves an incorrigibility requirement, which can be partly expressed by saying that 'I know, but I may be wrong' is an improper expression, the question then arises: if I require incorrigibility for the proper use of 'I know' and yet refuse to apply as standards of incorrigibility standards of evidence socially and normally *justifying my saying* 'I know', what do I take incorrigibility to consist of? How does one conceive an incorrigible statement as distinct from statements, say, with few and remote sources of error?

So far as I can judge, there are no criteria by which we can make the distinction, at least none that would guarantee correct results.[1] Remember that standards allowing any sources of error whatsoever would have to be rejected.

But, then, if incorrigibility is (practically) inconceivable in every concrete case, we have to ask ourselves whether the requirement is *unwarranted*. Since it is impossible to satisfy, surely this requirement functions no differently from any other requirement that makes 'I know' useless, that is, that prevents any correct use or occurrences of 'I know' whatsoever? Could we not, for example, just as well require that *p*, in 'I know that *p*', be green, square, and smell of jasmin? The effect would be the same —or perhaps better in so far as we would not lead innocent people, with little ability to see sources of error, into misusing the phrase 'I know'.

The relevance and strength of these reflections can be assessed more clearly if we first ask, in a preliminary way, where we are in the dialogue, what stage we have reached. It seems that we are not here considering something that implies criticism of uses of 'I know' satisfying normal, social standards. We have already concluded that all such standards sometimes break down, or at least are liable to break down.

We have in fact branched off from the usual discussions in concrete cases where mistakes are supposed to be detected and standards modified, and have entered upon a study and discussion of the implications of the view that the expression 'I know, but I may be wrong' is improper. In fact, we are now taking a broad view which comprehends both experience of past mistakes and the implications of the impropriety of the expression 'I know, but I may be wrong'. The transition to this viewpoint is effected in the light of the history of supposed mistakes. And this is, of course, an undertaking and a purpose *different* from the usual, normal, or everyday. What we are interested in may be stated in various ways, one of them thus: Errors, for instance, in geometry and in the historical development of the calculus of probability, have cropped up in a completely unpredicted way; judgments proclaiming that an error has been found have in some cases been retracted, in

<hr/>

[1] Stock answers would be to say that if the statement is true by convention, logically true, necessarily true, analytic, or *a priori*, it is incorrigible. But the conventions referred to are mostly obscure and the relation between a convention and the statements said to be true by that convention complicated and far from 'self-evident'. (And do statements which are true *solely* by convention express knowledge?) Similar things hold good of the criteria that a statement is necessarily true, analytic, or *a priori*.

other cases such judgments continue to be upheld. For example, in this century a large-scale reversal of judgments has affected Stoic logic. Because it was interpreted by Prantl and others in the light of Aristotle, we now say that Stoic logic was misjudged. Consider, too, the case of Aristotelian physics. Here there has been a shift (broadly speaking) from acceptance of it as true to a vehement rejection of it as false, and then a shift towards a kind of relativism, according to which if certain modern postulates and definitions are accepted there are many plain falsehoods, but if Aristotle's own are used there are less.[1] More often than oscillation from true to false and from false to true, painstaking studies reveal incomparabilities: a sentence T_0 is given various interpretations T_1, T_2, . . . and one generation accepts T_0 in the sense of T_1, another rejects T_0 in the sense of T_2. How the first generation would react to T_2 and the second to T_1 is not known. The sources of incomparability are as unpredictable as those of error and affect the use of 'I know that p' just as heavily.

It is my impression that in the course of intense studies of *reversals of judgments* interculturally and down the centuries, the application of the known *vs.* not-known distinction becomes *unwise*. That is, the use of this distinction in daily life does not itself furnish acceptable grounds for saying in such contexts 'I know' in some cases and 'I do not know' in others. Besides that, the usual incentives for saying such things disappear. Let us see how this might be.

Starting out from everyday-life situations, one may in a perfectly natural way be led to discuss reversals of judgment in general, and from that to reversals of judgment in systematic research. What, at this stage, would be the reasons for applying the phrases 'I know' and 'I do not know'?

One could begin to apply some normal standards for 'I know' and 'I do not know' in historical narrative or elsewhere, and those standards the specialist on human failures would himself claim to satisfy—in the loose way he considers this to be done normally. But what if someone questions him as a fellow-student, at the same stage of the debate?

Well, first of all, we note that 'I know' has a performative func-

[1] Cf. Kuhn, T. S., *The Structure of Scientific Revolutions* (University of Chicago Press, Chicago, 1962). The basic sceptical and relativist framework of this book has been clearly pointed to by P. K. Feyerabend in 'Problems of Empiricism', in R. G. Colodny (Ed.), *The Edge of Certainty* (Prentice-Hall, Englewood Cliffs, N.J., 1965). See p. 250.

tion conjoined with the cognitive, and this function is, as we have seen, inessential, irrelevant, or even disturbing in research communication: one researcher does not *vouch* for a (research) statement which the other then makes use of on the basis of trust. In fact, the situation could easily become ridiculous if the fellow-student insisted on using 'I know' or 'I do not know'. In short, there is less *incentive* here for using 'I know that *p*' at the stage of discussion we are now considering.

Secondly, even if there were an incentive, how could the conceptual framework erected during the debate be pressed to yield a basis for the use of 'I know'? Such a basis is destroyed by concentration on the truth requirement, by the resulting explication of the incorrigibility requirement, and by the detection of sources of error.

Perhaps it will be objected that this latter is a 'mere' psychological account of inapplicability. But whatever the suggested demerits of this, the facts still provide the basis of a rational reconstruction. It is possible to construct rules for reasonable limits of the distinction's application under variation of definiteness of intention, or to develop framework rules, the changes of framework being in turn correlated to stages of a dialogue.

We have raised the question 'Can the incorrigibility requirement ever be satisfied?', and the answer proposed is a 'No', but with an essential qualification. The question belongs to a stage of a dialogue at which the standard requirements for justifiably denying 'I may be wrong' are out of place, that is, where the rules regulating the propriety of the opposition of 'I know' and 'it cannot be wrong' are no longer applicable. In their place there is an unsatisfiable requirement that there should be no sources of error. Unsatisfiable not because the requirement is unintelligible or nonsensical or because this can be derived from some kind of logical or other necessity; in my own case at least the basis for stating 'It cannot be satisfied' is a study of proposed examples of incorrigible statements. How this basis is to be classified methodologically, I must here leave to others to decide.

There is another qualification. There are good reasons, though not, I think, decisive ones, for demanding a description of particular sources of error in criticizing a proposed incorrigible statement. On this view the claim for a statement's incorrigibility holds so long as no particular source of error is given. However, in many cases and especially in relation to negative examples ('I am *not* using the tail of a scorpion as a pen in writing this sentence', and the like) the sources will be ridiculously inadequate as *particular* sources of error. Perseverance in claiming corrigibility will then probably be found in some abstract considerations about sources of error, the chasm between evidence and the evidenced, a general fallibility in thinking. I say probably, because here it is a difficult question of motivation. So, if it is agreed that *particular, special* sources of error are to be enumerated for corrigibility to be substantiated, my conclusion would have to be that there *are* incorrigible statements but that they are of very special kinds, occurring neither in everyday life nor in science, but constructed for the very purpose of establishing the thesis that there are incorrigible statements.

It will be pointed out, however, that if incorrigibility cannot be realized, a requirement of incorrigibility will amount to a demand for the impossible. But can we rationally demand something impossible? It seems not. Then if it is irrational to demand the impossible, to require incorrigibility is a case of irrationality. And it might be concluded that therefore scepticism is irrational, because conclusions such as 'We cannot know anything' will have at least one premise which is irrational; and because we are aiming at being rational, the conclusions will have to be rejected.

What are we to make of this argument? Well, it seems clear that it would be of value only to an opponent who does *not* require incorrigibility, who is satisfied with what he *can* attain. For one could scarcely accuse the sceptic of irrationality unless one could show that there was a rational alternative in which incorrigibility was not required. Otherwise one would surely have to concede the sceptic his argument rather than criticize it.

However, it is not entirely accurate to say that the sceptic himself is demanding the impossible. All he states is that those who insist on using 'I know that *p*', and who also require incorrigibility as a requirement of the known, demand the impossible. At the same time he would contend that a clear-cut explicit renunciation of incorrigibility leads to contradictions or to intolerable divergences from the established usage of 'I know that *p*', an argument which we have tried to substantiate in the previous chapter.

Arthur Pap summarizes his own and G. E. Moore's antisceptical position in a few words. The *real existence* of the external world is established roughly as follows: I hold up my right hand; I see it, you see it, hence my right hand really exists; hence the external world really exists. But the Pyrrhonist would quite happily partici- pate in a discussion, say, about whether this or that war veteran has a right hand or not. He is not a particularly diffident or mis- trustful sort of person and might even believe and trust the testi- mony of others without seeing the man in question. But the term 'real existence' is commonly associated with technical philosophic terminologies. It is here that the Pyrrhonist's suspension of judg- ment enters the picture. Given professional definitions of 'real existence', 'hand', 'my', 'see', 'hence', 'world', etc., the Pyrrhonist is one who is likely to find himself unable to find one professional opinion more convincing than another. Pap adds:

'The question which the skeptic ought to be able to answer is: *what would it be like* to know for certain that the objects we perceive really exist, in other words, what do you, skeptic, *mean* by the phrase "I know for certain that *x* really exists?" That you cannot be using the phrase the way common sense uses it is evident from the fact that your disagreement with common sense is not a *factual* one, i.e. one that could in principle be settled by making further observations. No matter how many corroborating tests we may adduce as proof for the real existence of our hands, the skeptic still is not convinced.'[1]

In his answer the sceptic would stress that he listens to dogma- tists in order to understand the statement 'I know for certain that *x* really exists'. Surveying the various conceptualizations offered, however, there has not as yet been any *x* such that he, the sceptic, finds it certain and true that *x* really exists. But this does not pre- clude the sceptic from exhibiting trust and confidence in his or anyone else having two hands. And it will be up to the dogmatist to prove that trust and confidence implies adherence to a con- ceptualization concerning the real existence of an external world.

Pap attempts, he says, 'to show that the proposition, doubted by the Cartesian skeptic, "there exists an external world" can be known with certainty by observing the way words are commonly used'. His argument runs as follows:

'Hence only one conclusion can be drawn: the skeptic must use the phrase "Knowing for certain that *x* really exists" in some very special sense, and as long as he does not explain what that sense is, we may as well assume that the statement "we can never know for certain that any

[1] *Elements of Analytic Philosophy* (Macmillan, New York, 1949), pp. 147–8.

physical objects really exist and are not mere dream images" is either false or else meaningless.'[1]

If a man remains unconvinced after inspecting a long list of arguments in favour of the real existence of an external world *in the sense (or senses) of Cartesian dualism*, to my mind he deserves to be congratulated. But to conclude that the sceptic must use the phrase 'knowing for certain that *x* really exists' in some very special sense is wholly gratuitous. Indeed, in elaborating Cartesian concepts of real existence and the external world, one obtains very special senses, high-degree precizations of everyday terms, many of them transintentional in relation even to most professional epistemologists. The sceptic's position in respect of these is that he is faced with alternative directions of precization and he sees no convincing argument why he should choose any one of them. As for the appeal to ordinary usage, that is beside the point: here the sceptic is entitled to insist on the unwarrantedness of applying any clear-cut conceptualized distinction between knowing and not knowing.

It seems that Pap disregards the long and difficult path from believing somebody has a right hand, and has not lost it, to asserting propositions, positive or negative, concerning the real existence of something. Otherwise he would not be so optimistic as to try to show by noting the way in which words are commonly used that the Cartesian dogmatist (as an opponent of the Cartesian sceptic) is right.

In short, it seems that the sceptic's position is in no way affected by the unsatisfiability of the incorrigibility requirement. On the other hand, it must be remembered that where we talk in terms of incorrigibility we are applying the known *vs.* not-known distinction at a stage in the dialogue where the conclusion that incorrigibility is impossible no longer implies criticism of uses of 'I know' satisfying normal, social standards. As far as these latter are concerned, this whole question of whether incorrigibility is possible or not does not arise. The relation here between ordinary uses of the distinction and uses in the extended stages of the dialogue can be aptly described in terms of C. D. Broad's definition of a 'silly theory': 'By a "silly" theory I mean one which may be held at the time when one is talking or writing professionally, but which only an inmate of a lunatic asylum would think of

[1] *Elements of Analytic Philosophy*, p. 148.

carrying into daily life.'[1] The incorrigibility *formulations* and *formulations* like 'I do not know anything', which can be accepted as expressing tenable conclusions provided certain qualifications are also accepted, have by these very qualifications an intended field of validity which explicitly *excludes* daily life. They cannot be carried over for the simple reason that if they should be, they would not be the same conclusions.

14. INCORRIGIBILITY OF TRUTH

We must include here a few words on the role of the notion of truth in creating disturbing problems about knowing.

The requirement that in order for me to know that p, p must be true, creates complications because the sense of 'true' here is a very demanding one. In order that I should know that p, p must be the case. The notion of a true statement implied here is well defined by Aristotle (especially if *esti* is translated by 'is the case'): true statements are statements which say about that which is the case that it is the case, false are those which say about that which is not the case that it is the case.

If it is the case that p, it cannot also be the case that not-p. The exclusiveness, the narrow path of truth, is also well taken care of when, following Aristotle, we link the notion of truth to his (so-called) principle of contradiction.

In ordinary, undisturbed discourse and thinking there is a seemingly stable insight into what is the case. Even in posing questions and doubting (about something definite) there are always some stable insights implied, some indubitable and direct access to what is the case. By requiring 'p must be the case', 'what is the case' (*der Sachverhalt*) becomes unrelated to our standards of evidence, our purposes of discussion, our standards of incorrigibility. Yet the notion of 'what is the case' is one that is very much alive.

Attempts to avoid the notion, exchanging it for the more, as it were, epistemically self-conscious notions of 'what is verified', 'statement with maximum probability', etc., easily break down, and in a way similar to concepts of knowing which try to do without a separate truth requirement: we generate the possibility of both p and not-p being true, or of p remaining true at one date

[1] *Mind and Its Place in Nature* (Routledge & Kegan Paul, London, 1925), p. 5.

147

and at a later date not-p being found to be true, and remaining true.[1]

15. CRITICAL INSPECTION OF ARGUMENTS IN FAVOUR OF INCORRIGIBILITY AS UNATTAINABLE

At this point there is a further possible objection to be faced. In asserting that incorrigibility requirements arise in view of experience of past mistakes we assume we are justified in stating that mistakes have occurred. But what justification for this is there? What justifies us in stating that the evidence for a mistake was of a high standard? And in making these statements, what kind of announcement do we make? If we claim to *know* all these things on which our critique of incorrigibility rests, surely there is an inconsistency somewhere? But if that is the case, are there not serious repercussions on the argumentation in the previous sections?

Let us first see what happens if the view that incorrigibility cannot be reached is expressed in the terminology of 'knowing'. Suppose the view goes as follows: ' "I know that p" is true only if it cannot be false that p, but I know that p may be false, that p is corrigible, that there is a source of error.' But the truth requirement can be applied to the latter statement too. Hence we get 'It cannot be false that I know that p may be false' and 'It cannot be false that I know that p is corrigible, that there is a source of error'. Now it would hardly be reasonable of the proponent of this view to accept these 'second-order' statements as incorrigible; to do so would be to falsify the view. And besides there seems no reason to suppose that they alone should be immune to sources of error. At the stage of the dialogue at which the first-order statements were rejected he will also reject those of the second order. That is, he will not consider their knowledge claim warranted— or better, he will abstain also in these cases from considering whether the known *vs.* not-known distinction is applicable.

What now are the repercussions upon his argument concerning

---

[1] I may say 'p was true, but is not true any longer'. Here the truth has not been corrected. It is still true that p was true. At time t, A says 'There is a rainbow toward the East', at time $t + 1$, B says 'You are wrong, there is no rainbow', at which A answers 'I was right. What I said was true, but is no longer true.' That is, if repeated now, the statement would be false. If 'It is true that p' is retracted, not the truth but the belief is said to have been wrong.

the first-order statements? Does it collapse, leaving the field to the advocates of cases of incorrigibility?

It does not collapse. The knowledge claim could be retracted (as an inadvertence), and a new mode of announcement adopted, any other mode of cognitive *relevance*. The mode of announcement need not be explicitly expressed. One may inform people, in a preface, that in what follows, certain convictions, beliefs, or hypotheses (etc.) are not put forward as assertions. Beliefs are good enough, and in forwarding a belief there is no implied incorrigibility claim. 'I believe that *p*, but I may be wrong', is perfectly consistent. The same holds good of 'I am convinced that *p*, but *p* may be wrong'. It is, as already pointed out, not necessary to prefix every contribution to the case against the attainability of incorrigible statements with an 'I believe that . . .' or some other announcement different from 'I know that'. It might be misconstrued: the point, of course, is not to inform people that I have this or that *belief*. Therefore a preface is better.

In short, the disbeliever in incorrigible statements is not handicapped in an argument because of his disbelief. He can have no wish to pretend, nor get any benefit cognitively by pretending, that his arguments are incorrigible, and he can without loss leave the 'knowing'-terminology and conceptual framework alone.

There is another objection to be faced by those who dispute examples of incorrigible statements, namely that in citing sources of error they are speciously removing themselves from the real situation and putting themselves, or the example, into an imaginary one. For instance, in countering Austin's telephone example we are simply inventing sources of error; as regards the pig, it is simply know that Austin did not have amateur magicians as acquaintances. All we are entitled to say is something like:

'Very well, I concede that the world happens to be such that these statements are incorrigible. But there are many nonexistent yet conceivable worlds, some of them highly exciting. In one of them the "telephone" was not a telephone and the "pig" suddenly exploded like a balloon, leaving a new smell, that of helium. If it was a pig, it was certainly a very peculiar one.'

The argument that sceptics must take the world as it is can be given the following form:
Given human standards of credulity and the frequency and manner of our being deceived, it does not affect the issue of

scepticism that other beings might have been more easily discouraged and so become sceptical. That they might be sceptical is of no more interest than is, for physical theory, the observation that if the earth had or developed a much greater mass than it in fact has we should not be able to walk.

This kind of attack is serious, but not altogether convincing. When the disbeliever in incorrigible statements points to a source of rather astonishing mistakes, the erratic behaviour of practical jokers or amateur magicians, it is his conviction that it is just *our* world that contains the source—and James Jeans and others *may* be right in their suspicion that there are few similar worlds in all the Milky Way. The more details which a believer in an example of an incorrigible statement hands out, the more concrete is the disbeliever able to make his indications of sources of error. They may be very far-fetched, and the believer will, I presume, always be able to modify his example so as to take care of a suggested source of error $n + 1$. But the sceptic is likely to conceive of a source $n + 2$. No conclusion of the debate is foreseeable, and the field remains divided between the contesting parties. It can also be pointed out that any insistence that the world must be taken 'as it is' itself implies a partial scepticism. The rejection of both Academic and total Pyrrhonian scepticism in British philosophy is a case in point. Its scepticism consists in its disbelief or doubt in styles of life, ways of experience, and views of the self and the universe, *Weltanschauungen*, that distinctly colour even everyday life. Our daily life is supposed to be something we all have in common, and in it words get their distinct meanings. It is therefore supposed to furnish a common inescapable, nontranscendable frame of reference. This in spite of poets', prophets', and philosophers' testimony to the contrary. Indeed, this testimony is taken not only to be highly suspicious but also misleading: whatever has been said to the contrary, all men live in exactly the same world, the world of common sense.[1]

---

[1] It would be interesting to hear the personal experiences of university philosophers on this issue. All too little has been said about the personal background from which in part different points of view may be *understood*. Some sort of personal understanding is perhaps a necessary condition when judging fundamental positions in philosophy. At the opening of my own common-sense and trivialism period I remember the shock I received looking at about 150 philosophers advancing towards the food (placed on a big table) at a congressional banquet. There were no characteristic differences in behaviour, looks, talk or speed corresponding to disagreements in their books. Later in life I believe I have seen so much dis-conformism behind conformism and behind strikingly similar ways of behaving and talking

In German philosophy, in Kantian and phenomenological trends, Pyrrhonian and Academic scepticism is also rejected, but the counterarguments are characteristically different from those of Austin and Ayer and others. Instead of an appeal to institutions of everyday life, there is an appeal to absolutely basic insights and principles which make doubt impossible *überhaupt*. The principle of identity, of contradiction, the axioms of mathematics, and similar highly uneveryday themes are embarked upon.

Husserl's famous refutation of scepticism (in his terminology) is worth considering even if it is directed against negative dogmatism (Academic scepticism in Sextus's terminology) rather than against the Pyrrhonist.[1]

A theory as a piece of knowledge is, according to Husserl, a kind of proposition that claims truth, is certain of its truth, and is justified in claiming truth. (One is reminded of the sets of three requirements for asserting 'I know that *p*'.) Theories such as 'There is no truth', 'There is no knowledge' deny something they must accept in order to claim what they do. They are inconsistent and the inconsistency can be proved.

From the point of view of the Pyrrhonist both the negative dogmatism of 'There is no knowledge' and the refutation by Husserl are open to the charge of rashness. Arguments about the necessary conditions for the possibility of a theory *überhaupt* are typical of philosophical arguments within formidable conceptual systematizations. The modern Pyrrhonist would, I think, point to the non-evident conditions for the possibility of constructing theories about necessary conditions. The development of theoretical phenomenology has exposed the intricate maze of questions surrounding concepts of evidence functioning to establish what Husserl calls 'the evident conditions of the possibility of a theory *überhaupt*'.

To those who believe in a universal everyday life or in certain basic insights, the testimony of Sextus Empiricus and others about mature sceptics with their complete suspension of judgment has to be rejected. The testimony must be *false*; the sceptic is suffering from self-deception.

---

[1] The following remarks refer to § 32 in *Logische Untersuchungen* (2nd edn., Max Niemeyer-Verlag, Halle, 1913), Vol. I.

---

in daily life that I am convinced of styles of life and general attitudes colouring every thing—including the kind of utterance I am making now.

16. PENULTIMATE CONCLUSION ON MODERN SCEPTICISM

We have examined arguments against the reasonableness of saying 'I know nothing' and against the assertion that there are no incorrigible statements. It appears, however, that there are circumstances making it reasonable to use expressions like 'I know nothing' and 'No statement is incorrigible'. The realization that even in mathematics and logic, as well as in sense-experience, statements are sometimes withdrawn and their negations asserted, sometimes even both assertion and negation withdrawn and the issue left undecided, gives the expressions a legitimate function in conveying an appreciation of the history of human error and of the reversal of truth claims. But such expressions do not function cognitively, that is, they do not serve to express conclusions for which a general validity is claimed. In fact, both for these expressions and the more radical ones of the Pyrrhonist it is hard to find any satisfactory role in epistemology or in philosophical systems in general, if only because they are apt to be self-defeating when expressed in the precise way proper to their use in philosophical discussions.

Our conclusions are therefore extremely qualified compared with those which would have been expected to emerge if our discussion had been firmly anchored in a set of precise definitions. They can be expressed as follows: (1) 'I know nothing' can be a reasonable assertion in certain circumstances, but it has to be understood in the context of the circumstances that make it reasonable. (2) There are no incorrigible statements, although it is only pertinent to attach significance to this in certain situations.

What needs to be stressed is the very special character of an endorsement of 'I know nothing' or of the inapplicability of the distinction between known and not known. The important point is this: the endorsement does not have consequences for the socially established standards of evidence, but reflects the socially accepted, indefinite fluctuability of standards. It relates to special categories of dialogues in which there is created a conceptual framework of a special kind. In relation to such dialogues, and only in relation to them, the endorsement of the extremist formulation is tenable.

However, the so-called sceptical position in current discussion is mostly interpreted precisely as having consequences for the

usual, that is, average standards. The so-called sceptic is a critic
of those standards and denies the justifiability of *any* knowledge
claim. Thus Douglas Arner, who has the sceptic conclude 'that
we never properly claim knowledge'.[1] The distinction between
verification and justification (stressed by Anfinn Stigen)[2] can be of
some help here. I justify a claim for definite purposes, facing
definite persons in definite situations. In doing so I may sometimes be rash, sometimes overcautious, the weight of evidence
being the same in all cases. The mores covering the transactions
take cognizance of series of failures, but they also take cognizance
of successes.

It would be irresponsible to spread the rumour indiscriminately,
that is, to any listener in any situation, that no statements are
incorrigible, that strictly speaking we know nothing, or know no
empirical statement[3] to be true. Or, on the basis of considerations
in the foregoing, that standards of evidence need a general uplift-
ing. Or, that one ought to stop talking in terms of knowing or
knowledge because the hazards are too great. These are highly
startling and 'significant' pronouncements which are certainly
misleading and without foundation in the foregoing conclusions.

There remain, however, results of interest to any serious student
not only of the social psychology, sociology, and other branches
of the non-formal (future?) sciences of knowledge but also to
anybody interested in contemplating human efforts to reach new
knowledge and to improve the quality of the knowledge they
have.

Some such results and hypotheses may—at the risk of repeating
what has already been said—be stated as follows:

1. There is within a community no *definite stable general* standard
of evidence that must be fulfilled in order to justifiably say 'I
know that *p*', where *p* is any statement that can be grammatically
inserted.

2. There is not even a definite stable particular standard for any
particular *p*, although there are approximations to stability. There
are, therefore, no 'usual' standards which most people most of the
time find satisfactory in their normal working, in contrast to

[1] 'On Knowing', *Philosophical Review*, Vol. LXVIII (1959), p. 87.
[2] 'Descriptive Analysis and the Sceptic', *Inquiry*, Vol. 4 (1961), No. 4, e.g. p. 266.
[3] We have not discussed various subclasses of statements (empirical, logical, mathematical, analytic, necessary) because the arguments are in the main unaffected by the differences.

'special' standards for special purposes. The fluctuations of standards are not exceptional happenings, but part of their normal working.

3. Two of the many factors influencing the level of standards for knowing are as follows:

(*a*) the stage and direction of the dialogue in which a particular statement occurs;

(*b*) the responsibilities and risks incurred if it should happen (should later be agreed upon) that *p* is false.

On the whole, the more closely the evidence is inspected, or the more failures of high relevance to *p* have been reported in previous stages of the dialogue, or the more divided the opinion about *p* happens to be among the participants in the dialogue, the higher the standard.

Further, the graver the risks and responsibilities, the higher the standards necessary to avoid being subjected to social retaliations in the case of failure.

Sets of rules or theoretical models can be constructed more or less fitting the occasional explicit rules already verbalized in the community and the actual behaviour of the individuals considered competent.

4. However the rules may be formed in detail, there should be one from which a prohibition of the expression 'I know, but I may be wrong' can be derived. That is, it is clearly the part of the function of 'I know that *p*' to vouch for or guarantee that *p* is true and not false. Therefore clear indication of a source of error may exclude the use of 'I know that *p*'.

5. If the competent user of language and well-adjusted individual perceives a source of error at the moment of using, or at the moment of forming words in which he might possibly include, an 'I know', he will not withhold 'I know' unless this source is of an important or probable kind; that is, only if it seems more or less likely that *p* will actually turn out to be false. Otherwise it is not *worth mentioning*. The situation for the users of 'I know' is different from that of the neutral (or more or less neutral) bystander who (1) studies the community and who (2) studies sources of error *independently* of the particular situation or interaction in which the utterer of 'I know' happens to be placed.

The bystander will normally find many sources of error which do not occur to the user of 'I know'. Some of these will be such that the user, upon being made aware of them, will ignore them, taking them to be of a completely negligible order of magnitude, or of a kind that all know of but implicitly agree to leave out of (almost any) consideration. ('There may be a war', 'The sun may not rise tomorrow', 'Our historical textbook may be completely wrong' etc.) Some will be embarrassing to the user of 'I know', not because the standards of the community are such that it should have occurred to him as a source of error, and should have made him abstain from using 'I know', but because he will normally take *any* source *occurring to him* as *ipso facto* a sufficient reason to refrain from using 'I know'. The bystander disturbs the delicate adjustment.

6. Nearly all cases in which an 'I know that *p*' is well placed are such that one might very well have *not* known that *p*. This means that platitudes are generally not introduced by 'I know that', but that, on the contrary, very many statements which to the bystander involve clear sources of error *are* thus introduced. It is therefore out of the question for him to take the actual use of 'I know' as conforming or even intending to conform to a rule of incorrigibility as understood and operated by a neutral bystander.

7. If he makes the sources and frequencies of error a subject of special study, the epistemologist *continues* dialogues (of a kind rarely observed in the community) with such a tenacity and stress on explicit conceptual frameworks that he must be considered a more or less neutral bystander rather than a member of the community in these matters.

At such stages of the dialogue on a given *p*, or on knowing in general, it is reasonable to hold that *no statement is incorrigible*, and that the known *vs.* not-known distinction decreases towards zero in applicability with increasing stress on defining knowing within a precise conceptual framework.

8. Among fellow epistemologists the results of the studies may well be expressed by 'I do not know anything' or 'Knowledge cannot be reached', but only as part of a report containing many reservations, qualifications, and stating some assumptions or postulates governing the study. Announced to the epistemologically innocent user of 'I know', and particularly in situations in which he is just making use of that phrase, the epistemological formulations are grossly misleading, inevitably being interpreted in ways that are not intended.

Thus, it seems to me that the study of 'I know' is not a profitless or pointless study, and that the interest of it is not reduced because the results are of no or little application to the so-called everyday life of the users of 'I know'. After all, the everyday life is not the life we live *every* day, and the limitation to the ordinary is itself extraordinary.

My conclusion on modern scepticism can be put as follows. If by scepticism or 'epistemological scepticism' is meant a doctrine expressible by 'There can be nothing known', 'No statement can be known to be true', or 'No empirical statement can be true' without essential and severe qualifications and reservations, then scepticism is untenable. If, however, the reservations and qualifications are made which are suggested in the foregoing, such scepticism is tenable. But its most adequate formulation, as I have tried to show, is in terms of the inapplicability of the known *vs.* not-known distinction in relation to any suitable explicit conceptual framework.

17. ULTIMATE CONCLUSION ON MODERN SCEPTICISM

The arguments I have offered both in this and the previous chapters are designed to give support to the Pyrrhonian sceptic. The discussion as a whole is an attempt, on the part of a sympathetic metasceptic, to defend the Pyrrhonist against various undeserved objections. Some of these objections can clearly be met, in the case of others it may be less obvious that a satisfactory answer has been provided. In some cases, perhaps even in most, it would be wrong to say the counterarguments against those who dispute the possibility, or plausibility, or sincerity, of scepticism were decisive. But of course the radical sceptic, too, would fail to find them decisive. Perhaps our own conclusions here should be genuinely sceptical. After all, the conclusion that there are no incorrigible statements might seem to be based on such doubtful case studies as to cast doubt on its tenability. It might be appropriate to wonder whether, if the requirements of evidence are that low, it might not be possible also to deny a thesis on the non-existence of incorrigible statements.

Yet another counterargument might detract from the acceptability of our conclusions. If our study of candidates for incorrigibility is based on our own experience of the correction of mistakes, we should note that every case of correction of a mistake is based on certain assumptions. If for '*p*' we insert '*q* is a mistake' in our formulae, we get statements such as 'I know that *q* is a mistake', and the incorrigibility requirement which at one stage in the dialogue was found to be unsatisfiable is once more applicable. We should not say 'I know that *q* is a mistake, but *q* may be true'.

If the incorrigibility requirement forces us to admit that no claim that a mistake has been known to occur can be accepted, it must be admitted that there is no *known* case of somebody having been mistaken in saying 'I know that *p*'. More correctly, 'I know that N.N. was mistaken when saying "I know that *p*"' is always to be rejected as a claim to know; the incorrigibility claim involved cannot be satisfied. The same holds good for 'I know I may be mistaken', 'I know the incorrigibility requirement cannot be satisfied', and of course, 'I know knowledge can never be reached'.

I must confess that there are arguments against my conclusions, and that my own arguments are not such as to compel acceptance, either in the reader or in their author, and certainly not in the mature sceptic. On the other hand, to be content with conclusions based on arguments so *obviously* incapable of winning the sceptic's acceptance would hardly be a convincing demonstration of the metasceptic's sympathy for his subject-matter.

BIBLIOGRAPHY

SOURCES

BAYLE, PIERRE, 'Pyrrho', in *Dictionnaire historique et critique*, P. Brunel, P. Humbert, etc., Amsterdam, Leide, La Haye, Utrecht, 1740; and in *The Dictionary Historical and Critical*, Engl. edn. (2nd edn.), printed for J. J. and P. Knapton, etc., London, 1734–8. See also *Pierre Bayle; Historical and Critical Dictionary*, Selections, translated and edited by R. H. Popkin, The Library of Liberal Arts, Bobbs-Merrill Co., Indianapolis and New York, 1965.

CICERO, *De Finibus bonorum et malorum*, with an English translation by H. Rackham, The Loeb Classical Library, W. Heinemann, London, 1951 (first printed 1914).

CICERO, *De Natura Deorum Academica*, with an English translation by H. Rackham, The Loeb Classical Library, W. Heinemann, London, 1951 (first printed 1933).

CICERO, *Academia*, with an English translation by H. Rackham, The Loeb Classical Library, W. Heinemann, London, 1951.

SEXTUS EMPIRICUS, *Outlines of Pyrrhonism*, with an English translation by R. G. Bury, The Loeb Classical Library, Sext. Emp. I, W. Heinemann, London, 1933.

SEXTUS EMPIRICUS, *Against the Logicians*, with an English translation by R. G. Bury, The Loeb Classical Library, Sext. Emp. II, W. Heinemann, London, 1935.

SEXTUS EMPIRICUS, *Against the Ethicists*, with an English translation by R. G. Bury, The Loeb Classical Library, Sext. Emp. III, W. Heinemann, London, 1936.

SEXTI EMPIRICI, *Opera, recensuit Hermannus Mutschmann*, Vol. I, Πυρρωνείων Ὑποτυπώσεων, with Greek text, libros tres continens, B. G. Teubner, Leipzig, 1912.

SEXTI EMPIRICI, *Opera, recensuit Hermannus Mutschmann*, Vol. III, *Adversus Mathematicos*, with Greek text, libros I–VI continens, ed. J. *Mau* indices ad. Vol. 1–3 adiecit K. *Zanácek*, B. G. Teubner, Leipzig, 1954.

SEXTI EMPIRICI, *Opera, recensuit Hermannus Mutschmann*, Vol. II, *Adversus dogmaticos*, libros quinque (*adv. mathem.*, VII–XI) continens, B. G. Teubner, Leipzig, 1914.

SEXTI EMPIRICI, *Opera, Graece et latine*, in two volumes, ed. by I. A. Fabricius, Editio emendatior, B. G. Teubner, Leipzig, 1840.

HUME, DAVID, *A Treatise of Human Nature*, ed. by Selby-Bigge, Clarendon Press, Oxford (1949), Bk. I, Pt. 4, Sect. 1. And *An Enquiry concerning Human Understanding*, ed. by Selby–Bigge, Clarendon Press Oxford, 1955.

DE MONTAIGNE, MICHEL E, 'L'Apologie de Raymond Sebond', in *Les Essais de Michel de Montaigne*, ed. by Pierre Villey, F. Alcan, Paris, 1922.

PASCAL, BLAISE, *Pensées*, Brunschvicg, edn., introd. and notes by Ch.-Marc Des Granges, Editions Garnier Frères, Paris (1951), No. 434.

POPKIN, RICHARD H., 'Skepticism', in *The Encyclopedia of Philosophy* ed. by Paul Edwards, Collier–Macmillan, London (1967), Vol. 7.

HISTORICAL AND SYSTEMATIC ACCOUNTS OF GREEK AND OTHER SCEPTICISM

BEVAN, EDWYN, *Stoics and Sceptics. Scientific Theory*, Clarendon Press, Oxford, 1913.

BROCHARD, VICTOR, *Les Sceptiques grecs*, F. Alcan, Paris, 1887.

CHISHOLM, RODERICK M., 'Sextus Empiricus and Modern Empiricism', *Philosophy of Science*, Vol. 8 (1941).

GOEDECKEMEYER, ALB., *Die Geschichte des griechischen Skeptizismus*, Dietrich, Leipzig, 1905.

HICKS, R. D., *Stoic and Epicurean*, Longmans, London (1910), Ch. 8.

MACCOLL, NORMAN, *The Greek Sceptics, from Pyrrho to Sextus*, London, 1869.

PATRICK, MARY MILLS, *Sextus Empiricus and Greek Scepticism*, Deighton Bell & Co., Cambridge, 1899.

POPKIN, RICHARD H., 'Berkeley and Pyrrhonism', *Review of Metaphysics*, Vol. V (1951-2), pp. 223–46.

POPKIN, RICHARD H., 'David Hume and the Pyrrhonian Controversy', *Review of Metaphysics*, Vol. VI (1952–3), pp. 65–81.

POPKIN, RICHARD H., 'David Hume: His Pyrrhonism and his Critique of Pyrrhonism', *Philosophical Quarterly*, Vol. I (1950–1), pp. 385–407. Reprinted in *Hume*, edited by V. C. Chappell, New York (1966), pp. 53–98.

POPKIN, RICHARD H., 'The High Road to Pyrrhonism', *American Philosophical Quarterly*, Vol. II (1965), pp. 1–15.

POPKIN, RICHARD H., *The History of Scepticism from Erasmus to Descartes*, University of Utrecht Publications in Philosophy, Van Gorcum & Co., Assen, 1960. Revised edition 1964.

POPKIN, RICHARD H., 'The Sceptical Crisis and the Rise of Modern Philosophy', Parts I, II, and III, *Review of Metaphysics*, Vol. VIII (1953–4), pp. 132–51, 307–22, 499–510.

POPKIN, RICHARD H., 'The Sceptical Precursors of David Hume', *Philosophy and Phenomenological Research*, Vol. XVI (1955), pp. 61–71.

RICHTER, RAOUL, *Der Skeptizismus in der Philosophie*, I, II, Dürr'sche Buchh., Leipzig, 1904.

ROBIN, LÉON, *Pyrrhon et le scepticisme Grec*, Presses Universitaires, Paris, 1944.

OTHER WORKS

AUSTIN, J. L., *Philosophical Papers*, Clarendon Press, Oxford, 1961.

AUSTIN, J. L., *Sense and Sensibilia*, Clarendon Press, Oxford, 1962.

AYER, A. J., 'Philosophical Scepticism', in *Contemporary British Philosophy*, ed. by H. D. Lewis, The Muirhead Library of Philosophy, Allen & Unwin, London, The Macmillan Co., New York, 1956.

AYER, A. J., *The Problem of Knowledge*, Penguin Books, London, 1956.

AYER A. J., 'A Reply to Mr. Stigen', *Inquiry*, Vol. 4, No. 4 (Winter 1961).

BEROFSKY, BERNARD, 'Minkus–Benes on Incorrigibility', *Mind*, Vol. 67, No. 266 (April 1958), pp. 264–6.

CASTAÑEDA, HECTOR–NERI, 'Knowledge and Certainty', *The Review of Metaphysics*, Vol. 18, No. 3 (March 1965).

CHISHOLM, RODERICK M., 'Theory of Knowledge', in *Philosophy* (The Princeton Studies), by Roderick M. Chisholm, Herbert Feigl, William K. Frankena, John Passmore, and Manley Thompson, Prentice-Hall, Englewood Cliffs, N. J. (1964), pp. 244–344. Cf. also Chisholm, Roderick M., *Theory of Knowledge*, Foundations of Philosophy Series, Prentice-Hall, Englewood Cliffs, N. J., 1966.

GULLVÅG, INGEMUND, *Truth, Belief and Certainty*, Det kgl. Videnskaps Selskaps Skrifter 1964, No. 2, Trondheim, 1964.

GULLVÅG, INGEMUND, 'Scepticism and Absurdity', *Inquiry*, Vol. 7, No. 2 (Summer 1964).

HARRISON, JONATHAN, 'Knowing and Promising', *Mind*, Vol. 71, No. 284 (October 1962).

HEGEL, G. W. F., *Phänomenologie des menschlichen Geistes*, Godhard, Bamberg, 1807.

HEGEL, G. W. F., *Vorlesungen über die Geschichte der Philosophie*, Vol. I, Verlag von Dunder & Humblot, Berlin, 1833.

HEINTZ, WERNER, *Studien zu Sextus Empiricus*. Schriften d. Königsberger gelehrt. Gesellschaft Sonderreihe Band 2, Niemeyer, Halle, 1932.

HOFFMEISTER, JOHANNES, *Wörterbuch der philosophischen Begriffe*, F. Meiner, Hamburg (1955), p. 562.

HÖNIGSWALD, RICHARD, *Die Skepsis in Philosophie und Wissenschaft*, *Wege zur Philosophie*. Schr. zur Einf. in das philos. Denken, No. 7, Göttingen, 1914.

JAMES, WILLIAM, 'The Will to Believe', in *Essays in Pragmatism*, Hafner Publishing Company, New York, 1957.

JASPERS, KARL, *Psychologie der Weltanschauungen*, 4th edn., Springer Verlag, Berlin, Göttingen, Heidelberg, 1954.

MANNHEIM, KARL, *Ideology and Utopia. An Introduction to the Sociology of Knowledge*, Routledge & Kegan Paul, London, 1946. Translated from the German, *Ideologie und Utopie* (Bonn, 1929), by Louis Wirth and Edward Shils.

NATORP, PAUL, 'Protagoras, Demokrit, Epikur und die Skepsis', *Forschungen zur Geschichte des Erkenntnis problems im Alterthum*, VIII, Hertz, Berlin, 1884.

PAPPENHEIM, EUGEN, *Erläuterungen zu des Sextus Empiricus Pyrrhoneïschen Grundzügen*, Philosophische Bibliothek, Erich Koschny (L. Heimann's Verlag), Leipzig, 1881.

PAPPENHEIM, EUGEN, *Der angebliche Heraklitismus des Skeptikers Ainesidemos*, 30 s. I. Teil, Berlin, 1889. (In *Wiss. Beil. zum Programm des Kölln. Gymn.* Berl., 1889.)

PAPPENHEIM, EUGEN, *Die Tropen der griechischen Skeptiker*, Chaps. I–III, § 6. *Wiss. Beil. zum Programm des Kölln. Gymn.*, Ostern, 1885.

PAPPENHEIM, EUGEN, 'Einleitung,' *Des Sextus Empiricus Pyrrhoneïsche Grundzüge*, Philosophische Bibliothek, Erich Koschny (L. Heimann's Verlag), Leipzig, 1877.

ROKEACH, MILTON, *The Open and Closed Mind*, Basic Books, New York, 1960.

RUSSELL, BERTRAND, *The Problems of Philosophy*, Oxford University Paperback Series, Oxford University Press, Oxford, 1956 (first published 1912).

RUSSELL, BERTRAND, *Human Knowledge : Its Scope and Limits*, George Allen & Unwin, London, 1948.

STIGEN, ANFINN, 'Descriptive Analysis and the Sceptic,' *Inquiry*, Vol. 4. No. 4 (Winter 1961).

STRAWSON, P. F., *Individuals. An Essay in Descriptive Metaphysics*, Methuen, London, 1959.

STRAWSON, P. F., 'A. J. Ayer's *The Problem of Knowledge*', a critical notice in *Philosophy*, Vol. 28 (1953).

THOMAS, L. E., 'Philosophic Doubt', *Mind*, Vol. 64, No. 255 (1955).

WAGNER, HANS, *Philosophie und Reflexion*, E. Reinhardt, München, 1959.

ZELLER, EDUARD, *Die Philosophie der Griechen in ihrer geschichtlichen Entwicklung dargestellt*, 3. Theil, 1. Abt., *Die nacharistotelische Philosophie*, 1. und 2. Hälfte, 2. Auflage, Fues' Verlag, Leipzig, 1865.

INDEX

International Library of Philosophy & Scientific Method

Editor: Ted Honderich
Advisory Editor: Bernard Williams

List of titles, page two

International Library of Psychology Philosophy & Scientific Method

Editor: C K Ogden

List of titles, page six

ROUTLEDGE AND KEGAN PAUL LTD
68 Carter Lane London EC4

International Library of Philosophy and Scientific Method
(Demy 8vo)

Allen, R. E. (Ed.)
Studies in Plato's Metaphysics
Contributors: J. L. Ackrill, R. E. Allen, R. S. Bluck, H. F. Cherniss, F. M.
Cornford, R. C. Cross, P. T. Geach, R. Hackforth, W. F. Hicken, A. C. Lloyd,
G. R. Morrow, G. E. L. Owen, G. Ryle, W. G. Runciman, G. Vlastos
464 pp. 1965. (2nd Impression 1967.) 70s.

Armstrong, D. M.
Perception and the Physical World
208 pp. 1961. (3rd Impression 1966.) 25s.
A Materialist Theory of the Mind
376 pp. 1967. about 45s.

Bambrough, Renford (Ed.)
New Essays on Plato and Aristotle
Contributors: J. L. Ackrill, G. E. M. Anscombe, Renford Bambrough,
R. M. Hare, D. M. MacKinnon, G. E. L. Owen, G. Ryle, G. Vlastos
184 pp. 1965. (2nd Impression 1967.) 28s.

Barry, Brian
Political Argument
382 pp. 1965. 50s.

Bird, Graham
Kant's Theory of Knowledge:
An Outline of One Central Argument in the *Critique of Pure Reason*
220 pp. 1962. (2nd Impression 1965.) 28s.

Brentano, Franz
The True and the Evident
Edited and narrated by Professor R. Chisholm
218 pp. 1965. 40s.

Broad, C. D.
Lectures on Psychical Research
Incorporating the Perrott Lectures given in Cambridge University in 1959
and 1960
461 pp. 1962. (2nd Impression 1966.) 56s.

Crombie, I. M.
An Examination of Plato's Doctrine
I. Plato on Man and Society
408 pp. 1962. (2nd Impression 1966.) 42s.
II. Plato on Knowledge and Reality
583 pp. 1963. (2nd Impression 1967.) 63s.

Day, John Patrick
Inductive Probability
352 pp. 1961. 40s.

2

International Library of Philosophy and Scientific Method
(Demy 8vo)

Edel, Abraham
Method in Ethical Theory
379 pp. 1963. 32s.

Flew, Anthony
Hume's Philosophy of Belief
A Study of his First "Inquiry"
296 pp. 1961. (2nd Impression 1966.) 30s.

Fogelin, Robert J.
Evidence and Meaning
Studies in Analytical Philosophy
200 pp. 1967. 25s.

Gale, Richard
The Language of Time
256 pp. 1967. about 30s.

Goldman, Lucien
The Hidden God
A Study of Tragic Vision in the *Pensées* of Pascal and the Tragedies of
Racine. Translated from the French by Philip Thody
424 pp. 1964. 70s.

Hamlyn, D. W.
Sensation and Perception
A History of the Philosophy of Perception
222 pp. 1961. (3rd Impression 1967.) 25s.

Kemp, J.
Reason, Action and Morality
216 pp. 1964. 30s.

Körner, Stephan
Experience and Theory
An Essay in the Philosophy of Science
272 pp. 1966. 45s.

Lazerowitz, Morris
Studies in Metaphilosophy
276 pp. 1964. 35s.

Linsky, Leonard
Referring
152 pp. 1967. about 28s.

Merleau-Ponty, M.
Phenomenology of Perception
Translated from the French by Colin Smith
487 pp. 1962. (4th Impression 1967.) 56s.

3

Perelman, Chaim
The Idea of Justice and the Problem of Argument
Introduction by H. L. A. Hart. Translated from the French by John Petrie
224 pp. 1963. 28s.

Ross, Alf
Directives, Norms and their Logic
192 pp. 1967. about 25s.

Schlesinger, G.
Method in the Physical Sciences
148 pp. 1963. 21s.

Sellars, W. F.
Science, Perception and Reality
374 pp. 1963. (2nd Impression 1966.) 50s.

Shwayder, D. S.
The Stratification of Behaviour
A System of Definitions Propounded and Defended
428 pp. 1965. 56s.

Skolimowski, Henryk
Polish Analytical Philosophy
288 pp. 1967. 40s.

Smart, J. J. C.
Philosophy and Scientific Realism
168 pp. 1963. (3rd Impression 1967.) 25s.

Smythies, J. R. (Ed.)
Brain and Mind
Contributors: Lord Brain, John Beloff, C. J. Ducasse, Antony Flew,
Hartwig Kuhlenbeck, D. M. MacKay, H. H. Price, Anthony Quinton and
J. R. Smythies
288 pp. 1965. 40s.

Science and E.S.P.
Contributors: Gilbert Murray, H. H. Price, Rosalind Heywood, Cyril Burt,
C. D. Broad, Francis Huxley and John Beloff
320 pp. about 40s.

Taylor, Charles
The Explanation of Behaviour
288 pp. 1964. (2nd Impression 1965.) 40s.

Williams, Bernard, and Montefiore, Alan
British Analytical Philosophy
352 pp. 1965. (2nd Impression 1967.) 45s.

International Library of Philosophy and Scientific Method
(Demy 8vo)

Wittgenstein, Ludwig
Tractatus Logico-Philosophicus
The German text of the *Logisch-Philosophische Abhandlung* with a new
translation by D. F. Pears and B. F. McGuinness. Introduction by Bertrand
Russell
188 pp. 1961. (3rd Impression 1966.) 21s.

Wright, Georg Henrik Von
Norm and Action
A Logical Enquiry. The Gifford Lectures
232 pp. 1963. (2nd Impression 1964.) 32s.

The Varieties of Goodness
The Gifford Lectures
236 pp. 1963. (3rd Impression 1966.) 28s.

Zinkernagel, Peter
Conditions for Description
Translated from the Danish by Olaf Lindum
272 pp. 1962. 37s. 6d.

International Library of Psychology, Philosophy, and Scientific Method
(Demy 8vo)

PHILOSOPHY

Anton, John Peter
Aristotle's Theory of Contrariety
276 pp. 1957. 25s.

Bentham, J.
The Theory of Fictions
Introduction by C. K. Ogden
214 pp. 1932. 30s.

Black, Max
The Nature of Mathematics
A Critical Survey
242 pp. 1933. (5th Impression 1965.) 28s.

Bluck, R. S.
Plato's Phaedo
A Translation with Introduction, Notes and Appendices
226 pp. 1955. 21s.

Broad, C. D.
Scientific Thought
556 pp. 1923. (4th Impression 1952.) 40s.

Five Types of Ethical Theory
322 pp. 1930. (9th Impression 1967.) 30s.

The Mind and Its Place in Nature
694 pp. 1925. (7th Impression 1962.) 55s. See also Lean, Martin

Buchler, Justus (Ed.)
The Philosophy of Peirce
Selected Writings
412 pp. 1940. (3rd Impression 1956.) 35s.

Burtt, E. A.
The Metaphysical Foundations of Modern Physical Science
A Historical and Critical Essay
364 pp. 2nd (revised) edition 1932. (5th Impression 1964.) 35s.

6

International Library of Psychology, Philosophy, and Scientific Method

(Demy 8vo)

Carnap, Rudolf
The Logical Syntax of Language
Translated from the German by Amethe Smeaton
376 pp. 1937. (7th Impression 1967.) 40s.

Chwistek, Leon
The Limits of Science
Outline of Logic and of the Methodology of the Exact Sciences
With Introduction and Appendix by Helen Charlotte Brodie
414 pp. 2nd edition 1949. 32s.

Cornford, F. M.
Plato's Theory of Knowledge
The Theaetetus and Sophist of Plato
Translated with a running commentary
358 pp. 1935. (7th Impression 1967.) 28s.

Plato's Cosmology
The Timaeus of Plato
Translated with a running commentary
402 pp. Frontispiece. 1937. (5th Impression 1966.) 45s.

Plato and Parmenides
Parmenides' *Way of Truth* and Plato's *Parmenides*
Translated with a running commentary
280 pp 1939 (5th Impression 1964.) 32s.

Crawshay-Williams, Rupert
Methods and Criteria of Reasoning
An Inquiry into the Structure of Controversy
312 pp. 1957. 32s.

Fritz, Charles A.
Bertrand Russell's Construction of the External World
252 pp. 1952. 30s.

Hulme, T. E.
Speculations
Essays on Humanism and the Philosophy of Art
Edited by Herbert Read. Foreword and Frontispiece by Jacob Epstein
296 pp. 2nd edition 1936. (6th Impression 1965.) 32s.

Lange, Frederick Albert
The History of Materialism
And Criticism of its Present Importance
With an Introduction by Bertrand Russell, F.R.S. Translated from the German
by Ernest Chester Thomas
1,146 pp. 1925. (3rd Impression 1957.) 70s.

International Library of Psychology, Philosophy, and Scientific Method

(Demy 8vo)

Lazerowitz, Morris
The Structure of Metaphysics
With a Foreword by John Wisdom
262 pp. 1955. (2nd Impression 1963.) 30s.

Lean, Martin
Sense-Perception and Matter
A Critical Analysis of C. D. Broad's Theory of Perception
234 pp. 1953. 25s.

Lodge, Rupert C.
Plato's Theory of Art
332 pp. 1953. 25s.

The Philosophy of Plato
366 pp. 1956. 32s.

Mannheim, Karl
Ideology and Utopia
An Introduction to the Sociology of Knowledge
With a Preface by Louis Wirth. Translated from the German by Louis Wirth and Edward Shils
360 pp. 1954. (2nd Impression 1966.) 30s.

Moore, G. E.
Philosophical Studies
360 pp. 1922. (6th Impression 1965.) 35s. See also Ramsey, F. P.

Ogden, C. K., and Richards, I. A.
The Meaning of Meaning
A Study of the Influence of Language upon Thought and of the Science of Symbolism
With supplementary essays by B. Malinowski and F. G. Crookshank
394 pp. 10th Edition 1949. (6th Impression 1967.) 32s.
See also Bentham, J.

Peirce, Charles, *see* Buchler, J.

Ramsey, Frank Plumpton
The Foundations of Mathematics and other Logical Essays
Edited by R. B. Braithwaite. Preface by G. E. Moore
318 pp. 1931. (4th Impression 1965.) 35s.

Richards, I. A.
Principles of Literary Criticism
312 pp. 2nd edition. 1926. (17th Impression 1966.) 30s.

Mencius on the Mind. Experiments in Multiple Definition
190 pp. 1932. (2nd Impression 1964.) 28s.

Russell, Bertrand, *see* Fritz C. A.; Lange, F. A.; Wittgenstein, L.

International Library of Psychology, Philosophy, and Scientific Method
(Demy 8vo)

Smart, Ninian
Reasons and Faiths
An Investigation of Religious Discourse, Christian and Non-Christian
230 pp. 1958. (2nd Impression 1965.) 28s.

Vaihinger, H.
The Philosophy of As If
A System of the Theoretical, Practical and Religious Fictions of Mankind
Translated by C. K. Ogden
428 pp. 2nd edition 1935. (4th Impression 1965.) 45s.

Wittgenstein, Ludwig
Tractatus Logico-Philosophicus
With an Introduction by Bertrand Russell, F.R.S., German text with an English translation en regard
216 pp. 1922. (9th Impression 1962.) 21s.
For the Pears-McGuinness translation—*see page 5*

Wright, Georg Henrik von
Logical Studies
214 pp. 1957. (2nd Impression 1967.) 28s.

Zeller, Eduard
Outlines of the History of Greek Philosophy
Revised by Dr. Wilhelm Nestle. Translated from the German by L. R. Palmer
248 pp. 13th (revised) edition 1931. (5th Impression 1963.) 28s.

PSYCHOLOGY

Adler, Alfred
The Practice and Theory of Individual Psychology
Translated by P. Radin
368 pp. 2nd (revised) edition 1929. (8th Impression 1964.) 30s.

Eng, Helga
The Psychology of Children's Drawings
From the First Stroke to the Coloured Drawing
240 pp. 8 colour plates. 139 figures. 2nd edition 1954. (3rd Impression 1966.) 40s.

Jung, C. G.
Psychological Types
or The Psychology of Individuation
Translated from the German and with a Preface by H. Godwin Baynes
696 pp. 1923. (12th Impression 1964.) 45s.

International Library of Psychology, Philosophy, and Scientific Method
(Demy 8vo)

Koffka, Kurt
The Growth of the Mind
An Introduction to Child-Psychology
Translated from the German by Robert Morris Ogden
456 pp. 16 figures. 2nd edition (revised) 1928. (6th Impression 1965.) 45s.
Principles of Gestalt Psychology
740 pp. 112 figures. 39 tables. 1935. (5th Impression 1962.) 60s.

Malinowski, Bronislaw
Crime and Custom in Savage Society
152 pp. 6 plates. 1926. (8th Impression 1966.) 21s.
Sex and Repression in Savage Society
290 pp. 1927. (4th Impression 1953.) 28s
See also Ogden, C. K.

Murphy, Gardner
An Historical Introduction to Modern Psychology
488 pp. 5th edition (revised) 1949. (6th Impression 1967.) 40s.

Paget, R.
Human Speech
Some Observations, Experiments, and Conclusions as to the Nature, Origin, Purpose and Possible Improvement of Human Speech
374 pp. 5 plates. 1930. (2nd Impression 1963.) 42s.

Petermann, Bruno
The Gestalt Theory and the Problem of Configuration
Translated from the German by Meyer Fortes
364 pp. 20 figures. 1932. (2nd Impression 1950.) 25s.

Piaget, Jean
The Language and Thought of the Child
Preface by E. Claparède. Translated from the French by Marjorie Gabain
220 pp. 3rd edition (revised and enlarged) 1959. (3rd Impression 1966.) 30s.

Judgment and Reasoning in the Child
Translated from the French by Marjorie Warden
276 pp. 1928 (4th Impression 1966.) 28s.

The Child's Conception of the World
Translated from the French by Joan and Andrew Tomlinson
408 pp. 1929. (4th Impression 1964.) 40s.

International Library of Psychology, Philosophy, and Scientific Method (Demy 8vo)

Piaget, Jean (continued)

The Child's Conception of Physical Causality
Translated from the French by Marjorie Gabain
(3rd Impression 1965.) 30s.

The Moral Judgment of the Child
Translated from the French by Marjorie Gabain
438 pp. 1932. (4th Impression 1965.) 35s.

The Psychology of Intelligence
Translated from the French by Malcolm Piercy and D. E. Berlyne
198 pp. 1950. (4th Impression 1964.) 18s.

The Child's Conception of Number
Translated from the French by C. Gattegno and F. M. Hodgson
266 pp. 1952. (3rd Impression 1964.) 25s.

The Origin of Intelligence in the Child
Translated from the French by Margaret Cook
448 pp. 1953. (2nd Impression 1966.) 42s.

The Child's Conception of Geometry
In collaboration with Bärbel Inhelder and Alina Szeminska. Translated from the French by E. A. Lunzer
428 pp. 1960. (2nd Impression 1966.) 45s.

Piaget, Jean and Inhelder, Bärbel
The Child's Conception of Space
Translated from the French by F. J. Langdon and J. L. Lunzer
512 pp. 29 figures. 1956 (3rd Impression 1967.) 42s.

Roback, A. A.
The Psychology of Character
With a Survey of Personality in General
786 pp. 3rd edition (revised and enlarged 1952.) 50s.

Smythies, J. R.
Analysis of Perception
With a Preface by Sir Russell Brain, Bt.
162 pp. 1956. 21s.

van der Hoop, J. H.
Character and the Unconscious
A Critical Exposition of the Psychology of Freud and Jung
Translated from the German by Elizabeth Trevelyan
240 pp. 1923. (2nd Impression 1950.) 20s.

Woodger, J. H.
Biological Principles
508 pp. 1929. (Reissued with a new Introduction 1966.) 60s.

11

867 PRINTED BY HEADLEY BROTHERS LTD 109 KINGSWAY LONDON WC2 AND ASHFORD KENT